THE PROCRASTINATION CURE

21 PROVEN TACTICS FOR CONQUERING YOUR INNER PROCRASTINATOR, MASTERING YOUR TIME, AND BOOSTING YOUR PRODUCTIVITY!

DAMON ZAHARIADES

ARTOFPRODUCTIVITY.COM

CONTENTS

Other Books by Damon Zahariades   v

Your Free Gift   1
Notable Quotables About Procrastination   3
Introduction: What Is Procrastination?   4
My Life As A Chronic Procrastinator   8
The Personal And Professional Price Of   11
Procrastination
What You'll Learn In The Procrastination Cure   16
How To Get Maximum Value Out Of This Book   19

PART I
WHY WE PROCRASTINATE

Fear Of Failure   23
Fear Of Success   26
Perfectionism   29
A Feeling Of Overwhelm   32
Laziness   35
Boredom   38
Aversion To Hard Work   41
Negative Self-Talk   44
Low Tolerance For Adverse Events   47
Uncertainty About How (Or Where) To Start   50
Inability To Make Decisions   53
Options That Promise More Immediate Gratification   56
No Immediate Consequences For Inaction   60
Pop Quiz: Are You A Habitual Procrastinator?   62

PART II
**21 WAYS TO BEAT YOUR INNER
PROCRASTINATOR**

Tactic #1: Eat The Frog First   69
Tactic #2: Do The First 10 Minutes   71
Tactic #3: Reward Yourself   73

Tactic #4: Fill Your Calendar   76

Tactic #5: Prioritize Tasks And Projects   78

Tactic #6: Shorten Your Daily To-Do List   82

Tactic #7: Apply Parkinson's Law   85

Tactic #8: Ask Others To Set Your Deadlines   87

Tactic #9: Leverage Your Peak-Energy Times Of Day   90

Tactic #10: Be Accountable To Someone   92

Tactic #11: Take Small Steps   94

Tactic #12: Avoid Boring Work (Whenever Possible)   98

Tactic #13: Get Rid Of Environmental Distractions   101

Tactic #14: Get Rid Of Digital Distractions   103

Tactic #15: Use The Time Chunking Method   106

Tactic #16: Eliminate As Many Unnecessary Tasks As Possible   109

Tactic #17: Focus On One Task At A Time   112

Tactic #18: Purge Negative Self-Talk   115

Tactic #19: Limit Your Options To One   118

Tactic #20: Figure Out Why You're Procrastinating   121

Tactic #21: Perform A Weekly Audit Of Your Goals   123

Bonus Tactic #1: Use Temptation Bundling   125

Bonus Tactic #2: Use Commitment Devices   128

Bonus Tactic #3: Forgive Yourself   131

PART III

WHEN PROCRASTINATION HELPS YOU TO GET THINGS DONE

The Art Of Active Procrastination   137

Bonus Material: Answers To Common Questions About Overcoming Procrastination   140

Final Thoughts On Conquering Procrastination   145

Did You Enjoy Reading The Procrastination Cure?   148

About the Author   151

Other Books by Damon Zahariades   153

OTHER BOOKS BY DAMON ZAHARIADES

∼

The Joy Of Imperfection: A Stress-Free Guide To Silencing Your Inner Critic, Conquering Perfectionism, and Becoming The Best Version Of Yourself!

Is perfectionism causing you to feel stressed, irritated, and chronically unhappy? Here's how to silence your inner critic, embrace imperfection, and live without fear!

∼

The Art Of Saying NO: How To Stand Your Ground, Reclaim Your Time And Energy, And Refuse To Be Taken For Granted (Without Feeling Guilty!)

Are you fed up with people taking you for granted? Learn how to set boundaries, stand your ground, and inspire others' respect in the process!

∼

Morning Makeover: How To Boost Your Productivity, Explode Your Energy, and Create An Extraordinary Life - One Morning At A Time!

Would you like to start each day on the right foot? Here's how to create quality morning routines that set you up for more daily success!

∼

Fast Focus: A Quick-Start Guide To Mastering Your Attention, Ignoring Distractions, And Getting More Done In Less Time!

Are you constantly distracted? Does your mind wander after just a few minutes? Learn how to develop laser-sharp focus!

∼

Small Habits Revolution: 10 Steps To Transforming Your Life Through The Power Of Mini Habits!

Got 5 minutes a day? Use this simple, effective plan for creating any new habit you desire!

∼

To-Do List Formula: A Stress-Free Guide To Creating To-Do Lists That Work!

Finally! A step-by-step system for creating to-do lists that'll actually help you to get things done!

∼

The 30-Day Productivity Plan: Break The 30 Bad Habits That Are Sabotaging Your Time Management - One Day At A Time!

Need a daily action plan to boost your productivity? This 30-day guide is the solution to your time management woes!

∼

The Time Chunking Method: A 10-Step Action Plan For Increasing Your Productivity

It's one of the most popular time management strategies used today. Double your productivity with this easy 10-step system.

Digital Detox: The Ultimate Guide To Beating Technology Addiction, Cultivating Mindfulness, and Enjoying More Creativity, Inspiration, And Balance In Your Life!

Are you addicted to Facebook and Instagram? Are you obsessed with your phone? Use this simple, step-by-step plan to take a technology vacation!

For a complete list, please visit

http://artofproductivity.com/my-books/

YOUR FREE GIFT

~

I'd like to give you something. It won't cost you a dime. It's my 40-page PDF action guide titled *Catapult Your Productivity! The Top 10 Habits You Must Develop To Get More Things Done*. It's short enough to read quickly, but meaty enough to offer actionable advice that can change your life.

I'd like you to have a copy with my compliments.

Claim your copy of *Catapult Your Productivity* by clicking the link below and joining my mailing list:

http://artofproductivity.com/free-gift/

Before we jump in, I'd like to express my thanks. I know your time is limited. I also realize there are numerous books and courses that promise to help you conquer procrastination.

You chose to read mine. That means the world to me. If you stick with me, I promise to make the time we spend together worthwhile.

In the pages that follow, you're going to learn how to finally overcome your tendency to procrastinate, and in doing so experience an exciting personal transformation.

NOTABLE QUOTABLES ABOUT PROCRASTINATION

You may delay, but time will not, and lost time is never found again.
- Benjamin Franklin

Procrastination is the thief of time, collar him.
- Charles Dickens

In delay, there lies no plenty.
- William Shakespeare

Only put off until tomorrow what you are willing to die having left undone.
- Pablo Picasso

INTRODUCTION: WHAT IS PROCRASTINATION?

~

E veryone procrastinates.

It's a universal temptation. Even productivity and time management experts, who are supposed to know better, regularly postpone taking action on things that require their attention. We're constantly enticed to put things off to pursue more appealing options.

For example, we persuade ourselves to forgo our daily visit to the gym, choosing instead to remain on the couch binge-watching our favorite Netflix shows. We ignore our lawns, which desperately need to be mowed, in favor of going to the theater to catch the latest blockbuster film. We choose to go out with our friends rather than study for an upcoming exam.

The question is, how can we lessen this tendency? Ultimately, how can we reduce its impact on our lives?

We can't eliminate it since our inclination to procrastinate is part of our nature. We tend to pursue what is easiest and most likely to deliver immediate gratification, even if doing so is inconsistent with our long-term goals.

The Procrastination Cure will give you the tools you need to overcome this inclination.

Before we go any further, however, it's important to understand what procrastination is, and by extension what it is *not*.

Procrastination Defined

Procrastination has traditionally been defined as postponing taking action on something in favor of doing something else. In this context, doing something else can mean doing nothing at all.

But this definition is insufficient. It fails to recognize circumstances in which putting things off is sensible and pragmatic.

For example, suppose you need to visit the grocery store. But it's Saturday afternoon and you know the store is likely to be swamped with customers. Unless you're in desperate need of something (for example, eggs or milk), it makes sense to postpone your visit until Monday afternoon. The store will be less crowded.

Is this an example of procrastination? In my opinion, defining it as such is overly simplistic. In truth, it's an example of practical time management.

So what constitutes true, life-impairing procrastination? Most of us grew up thinking it was the act of putting something off, and thus associate the habit with laziness. But as we saw in our "grocery store" example, laziness isn't the only reason to postpone a task.

earlier action

For the purpose of this book, we'll define procrastination as the act of deferring action on something when taking *earlier* action would arguably have been a better decision. For example, visiting the gym instead of binge-watching Netflix; mowing the lawn instead of going to the movies; studying for an upcoming exam instead of going out with friends.

The Procrastination Cure will show you how to make better decision between competing tasks and opportunities, and thereby increase your productivity and better manage your time.

Long-Term Goals Vs. Instant Gratification

As you'll see in *Part I: Why We Procrastinate*, there are numerous triggers for the procrastination habit. But the overarching reason we put things off is because something else promises to be more gratifying within a shorter time frame.

In short, we prefer doing things that deliver immediate gratification, even if we value the future benefits associated with addressing more important tasks. We prefer *present* rewards to future rewards. This is the case even if the latter are greater in scope.

For example, we purchase a new car knowing we should instead put the money into a retirement fund. We hang out with friends knowing we should instead study for an exam. We watch our favorite TV shows knowing we should instead go to the gym.

There's no way to short-circuit this preference for present rewards over future rewards. This preference is part of our nature. But we can use this knowledge to train ourselves to overcome our tendency to procrastinate. The trick is to make the benefits of taking action *more immediate*.

One way to do is this is through a strategy called temptation bundling, which we'll explore in detail in *Part II: 21 Ways To Beat Your Inner Procrastinator*.

The Curious Effect Of Taking Action

The biggest challenge in working on a task you consider to be boring, difficult, or unappealing, is *starting* on it. But a strange things happens once you start: the anxiety and dread associated with it rapidly declines.

Think about the last time you postponed an unappealing task

(for example, mowing your lawn, cleaning your bathroom, working on a report for your boss, etc.). The task probably nagged at you. Worse, the discomfort you felt probably grew the longer you postponed taking action.

What happened when you finally started working on the dreaded task? The discomfort and anxiety you felt, much of it stemming from the guilt of procrastinating, likely dissipated. Moreover, once you started working on it, you probably found it easy to continue doing so.

Here's a personal example:

I write for a living. But I don't always look forward to it. Writing a book, or even a comprehensive blog post, entails a lot of work. So, yes, I've been known to procrastinate.

But I've found that once I write the first 100 words - that's less than half a page - it's much easier to press onward and write the next 1,000, 2,000, or even 5,000 words.

Taking action causes the discomfort and guilt associated with procrastination to evaporate. It also erases the stress and worry of doing the task. And just as importantly, it gives us the momentum we need to continue working until the task has been completed.

In the next section, I'll describe how procrastination negatively affected my life, and what happened when I finally overcame it. My hope is that you'll relate to the challenges I describe, and be inspired to make a positive change in your own life.

MY LIFE AS A CHRONIC PROCRASTINATOR

~

My past is as close to a perfect case study in procrastination as you're likely to find. I was an extreme case. I practically earned a doctorate in the subject from the School of Hard Knocks.

Don't take my word for it. Judge for yourself. Here's a snapshot of my life many years ago...

I would send in my car registration late each year, resulting in fines. Why? Because writing a check and putting a stamp on an envelope (this was pre-internet) was apparently too much trouble for me. More than once, because my license plate lacked the appropriate registration sticker from the California Department of Motor Vehicles (DMV), I'd discover that my car had been towed.

Worse, there were times when I'd receive my new registration card and sticker from the DMV, and let both sit in my office for months on end. Remember, I was a chronic procrastinator. I apparently couldn't be bothered with actually putting the sticker on my license plate. The result? More fines and towing charges.

This tendency to postpone things - important things! - extended into every area of my life. I paid my car insurance bills late. I waited until I had no clean clothes before desperately doing a load of laundry. I postponed ending relationships, allowing them to drag on long after it was clear they were terminal.

In college, I postponed studying for tests. I waited until the last minute before working on class assignments. My friends knew that it practically took an act of Congress to get me to return their phone calls.

After college, I entered Corporate America and continued the same shenanigans. I postponed working on important projects. I waited until the last possible moment before turning in reports to my boss. I'd skip meetings - not because of a conscious decision to do so, but because I deferred the decision until the meetings had already started. At that point, I'd simply disregard them.

The fact that my career progressed in spite of such foolishness baffles me, and probably doesn't speak well of Corporate America.

I eventually left the corporate world, and ventured out on my own. But I hadn't kicked my procrastination habit, and was thus continually plagued by it. For example, I delayed creating new products for my customers and clients. I put off tracking my advertising expenses. I deferred researching new opportunities.

The result? My business suffered greatly for it.

What Happened After I Turned Things Around?

I eventually overcame my tendency to procrastinate. (We'll cover the tactics I used in *Part II: 21 Ways To Beat Your Inner Procrastinator*.) The effect has been nothing short of life-changing.

I experienced less anxiety and guilt. These feelings were replaced with confidence and purpose. I finally felt in control of my life.

By taking action more regularly, I was able to create more products, better manage my time, and improve my relationships (and end those that weren't working).

My productivity skyrocketed. I not only completed more work in less time, but I completed *important* work - the type that moved the needle with respect to my long-term goals.

Today, I still put things off on occasion. My inner procrastinator still manages to rear its head now and again. But I've learned to control him. And that has made a remarkable difference in my life.

In the next section, we'll talk about the price you're paying for procrastination - in your personal life as well as your professional life.

THE PERSONAL AND PROFESSIONAL PRICE OF PROCRASTINATION

～

I t's safe to say you're interested in managing your time more effectively and increasing your productivity. That's the reason you're reading this book. To those ends, you know intuitively that every decision you make regarding how you spend your time imposes a cost.

For example, let's say you have two activities to choose from: activity A and activity B. You can't do both; you must choose one over the other. In this scenario, one activity becomes the opportunity cost of the other. If you choose activity A, you must forgo doing activity B. Choose B, and you won't be able to do A.

Therein lies the reason it's important to identify tasks and activities that complement your goals. You lack the time to do everything.

Consider this principle in the context of procrastination. Each time we procrastinate, we choose one activity over another. The problem is, the items we postpone never go away. They linger, demanding more and more attention as time passes.

For example, your lawn will continue to grow until you mow

it (or hire someone to mow it for you). Next week's exam, one for which you're unprepared, won't miraculously be cancelled. The bathrooms in your home aren't going to clean themselves.

These tasks must be addressed at some point. The longer you postpone them, the more urgent they become.

The price you pay for procrastination is not always immediate. The *true* cost becomes apparent via a ripple effect that expands the more you put things off. This ripple effect eventually impacts both your personal and professional lives.

The Cost Of Procrastination On Your Personal Life

Putting things off can negatively affect your personal life in four distinct areas:

1. Your relationships
2. Your finances
3. Your health
4. Missed opportunities

Following are some examples of each.

Your Relationships

Suppose you and your spouse have had a major disagreement that has left unresolved issues. You know these issues can only be settled by having a serious, and likely difficult, conversation. Postponing this conversation will only result in increasing resentment and emotional distance.

Or suppose you delay getting back to friends regarding an upcoming get-together. Doing so may result in your missing the chance to spend quality time with them.

Or suppose you postpone buying tickets to an upcoming

sporting event for you and your kids. The event sells out, causing considerable disappointment for your family.

Your Finances

Suppose you delay paying your credit cards. If you end up paying them late, you'll be charged late fines. You'll also put your credit status at risk.

Suppose you put off filing your taxes until the last possible moment. Then, an emergency prevents you from filing them on time. You'll be on the hook for late fees and failure-to-pay penalties. You might even trigger an audit.

Suppose you procrastinate making investment decisions. Doing so could result in huge losses if your current investments are on the wrong side of the market.

Suppose you delay setting money aside for your retirement. At age 65, you might find yourself without the funds you need to retire in comfort.

Your Health

Procrastination can even become a health risk. For example, suppose you put off visiting the doctor when you feel ill. If you're lucky, your body's immune system will take care of the problem on its own. On the other hand, the sick feeling might stem from a serious affliction that requires prompt medical attention. Putting off a visit to your doctor can have disastrous consequences.

Suppose you put off exercising. You tell yourself that you'll start a daily workout regimen soon, but refuse to make a commitment. The months pass without your taking action, setting the stage for atrophied muscles, increased body fat, and even cardiac decline.

Suppose you're in your 40s and delay scheduling a

colonoscopy. You risk allowing colorectal cancer, which grows slowly and can be treated successfully if detected early, to spread.

Suppose you defer taking action on everything to the point that you're under constant pressure as things come due and work piles up. The stress can negatively affect your body, mind, and behavior.

Missed Opportunities

We miss opportunities every day thanks to our tendency to procrastinate. For example, recall the last time you put off making a reservation at a trendy restaurant only to discover you had waited too long.

Have you ever waited to purchase airline tickets only to learn the prices had significantly increased? Or worse, all the flights were full, and you were forced to wait on standby, hoping someone would cancel at the last minute.

Suppose you delay booking a room at your favorite hotel for an upcoming vacation. You figure that you have plenty of time to do so, but find to your dismay that the hotel is now booked at full capacity.

Suppose your home needs a new roof. A reputable contractor extends an attractive discount based on his business being slow at the time. But you postpone taking action, and later find that the contractor is booked and the discount is no longer available.

The Cost Of Procrastination On Your Professional Life

Delaying taking action can also hurt your professional life in numerous ways.

For example, suppose you learn of a promising job position that you're perfectly suited for. But you wait too long to send in your resume. Consequently, the position is filled before you have an opportunity to interview for it.

Suppose you're in sales. You delay following up on leads, figuring you can contact them tomorrow or the following day with no ill effect. But your leads cool off quickly, becoming less receptive to your overtures. Or worse, when they don't hear from you, they give their business to your competition. That translates into fewer sales and decreased commissions. It might even dash your chances for a promotion.

Suppose you're responsible for creating a number of important reports for your boss. You regularly procrastinate on them, forcing you to scramble at the last minute. This habit can result in your delivering the reports late or passing along bad data stemming from avoidable errors. Neither scenario is likely to reflect well on your quarterly performance reviews.

Ultimately, procrastination is evident in our daily work habits. These habits dictate our productivity; the more we put things off, the less productive we become. Worse, it becomes increasingly difficult to manage our time effectively as the postponed tasks, along with their respective deadlines, pile up.

THE ABOVE EXAMPLES illustrate that the cost of procrastination can be much greater than is immediately apparent. The habit produces a ripple effect that can significantly impact our personal and professional lives.

You now know what's at stake. In the next section, we'll cover what you can expect to learn in *The Procrastination Cure*.

WHAT YOU'LL LEARN IN THE PROCRASTINATION CURE

∾

There are three distinct parts to *The Procrastination Cure*. As with my other books, I've organized the material with a specific purpose in mind.

I urge you to read the book from beginning to end the first time, particularly if you're familiar with some of the material. Why? Because much of what we'll cover in *Part II* builds on the material in *Part I*. Likewise, the advice you'll find in *Part III* builds on the advice you'll find in *Part II*.

Reading from beginning to end ensures you benefit fully from every section.

Keep in mind that procrastination is a difficult habit to break. As with any habit, the longer you allow it to persist, the more deeply rooted it becomes. So if you've been a lifelong procrastinator, breaking the habit may take weeks, or even months.

Given this, after you've read *The Procrastination Cure* in its entirety, and applied every tactic described in *Part II*, revisit sections on an "as needed" basis. I've organized the material to make doing so easy. Simply look through the expanded table of contents to find the section (or sections) you want to reread at any given time.

With that out of the way, let's take a quick tour through each of the three sections in *The Procrastination Cure*.

Part I

Resolving a problem requires knowing *why* the problem occurs. *Part I: Why We Procrastinate* explores this issue in detail. We'll discuss the most common reasons we procrastinate, some of which you're certain to recognize as personal triggers.

As you read *Part I*, realize you're not alone. I personally relate to several of the reasons highlighted in this section of *The Procrastination Cure*. I'll reveal which ones along the way, and explain how and why they affect me.

My goal is to help you to overcome them.

Part II

This is the main section of the book. Although it moves quickly, it's comprehensive. In *Part II: 21 Ways To Beat Your Inner Procrastinator*, you'll learn nearly two dozen proven tactics for curbing your procrastination habit.

We'll discuss each one individually, and explore why they work. Keep in mind, none of these strategies are meant to be applied exclusive of the others. You'll see the best results when you apply all of them together.

Part III

Procrastination isn't always bad. In fact, it's sometimes practical. To that end, there are times when it makes sense to embrace it rather than avoid it.

Part III: When Procrastination HELPS You To Get Things Done will explore the controversial idea of *active* procrastination. We'll talk about how it can improve your focus, allow you to better allocate your time, and under the right circumstances help you to get more things done.

Bonus Material

You may have questions related to overcoming procrastination after you've finished reading this book. I've added a bonus section to *The Procrastination Cure* to address the most common questions I've been asked about this topic.

Some of these questions are tangentially related to material covered in *Parts I, II,* and *III.* But they introduce unique circumstances that warrant attention.

Taking The First Step Of The Rest Of Your Life

We have a lot to cover in the following pages. But I promise we'll move quickly. That way, you'll be able to apply the advice as soon as possible and see measurable results.

If you're a chronic procrastinator, you'll undoubtedly recognize the negative effects the habit is having on your life. I urge you to make a commitment to conquering it. You'll find that once you curb the tendency to put things off, and train yourself to consistently take action, you'll feel in much greater control of your life.

In the next section, I'll show you how to get maximum value from *The Procrastination Cure*.

HOW TO GET MAXIMUM VALUE OUT OF THIS BOOK

∼

I n the previous section, I urged you to make a commitment to curbing the procrastination habit. In the event you deferred taking action on that advice, I'll avoid pointing out the irony.

The important thing to keep in mind is that no book, no matter how comprehensive or well-written, will effect change in the reader unless he or she is committed to that change.

So that's the first step to getting maximum value out of *The Procrastination Cure*. Commit.

The second step is to identify your personal challenges and obstacles. In *Part I: Why We Procrastinate*, we're going to talk about elements like fear, laziness, perfectionism, and negative self-talk. Acknowledge these challenges if they're present in your life. As I noted in the previous section, we need to know *why* a problem occurs before we can successfully address it.

The third - and arguably most important - step is to apply the strategies and tactics you'll learn about in *The Procrastination Cure*. Nearly everything you read in this book is designed to be implemented. Practical application is the quickest, surest way to see positive changes in your life. As you read *Part II* and *Part III*, do so with the willingness to take action on the advice.

The Procrastination Cure is short by design. Even the longer sections move at a quick pace. The goal is to help you move beyond *reading* and get to the *application stage* as quickly as possible.

This book will give you all of the tools and resources you'll need to control your inner procrastinator once and for all. Whether you're a CEO, student, entrepreneur, stay-at-home parent, salesperson, or freelancer, these methods work. And importantly, they'll work regardless of your personal circumstances.

If you're ready to start taking action on a consistent basis, and thereby rein in your inner procrastinator, let's get started.

First up: the most common reasons we procrastinate.

PART I

WHY WE PROCRASTINATE

~

To fully appreciate the reasons we procrastinate, it's important to distinguish between our present and future selves. They coexist, but are always in conflict with each other. There's a continuous disconnect between them because they're driven by entirely different things.

The Present Self is attracted to activities that promise immediate gratification. The Future Self is interested in activities that promise a "payoff" down the road.

For example, the Future Self is willing to exercise to get into shape. The Present Self would rather sit on the couch and watch television.

Once you understand the disassociation between these two parts of your identity, you'll fully appreciate the individual reasons you delay taking action.

This section of *The Procrastination Cure* will explore these reasons in detail. As we discuss each of them, consider how they affect the decision-making process between your present and future selves.

FEAR OF FAILURE

~

F ear plays a significant role in our tendency to procrastinate. It manifests in various ways, but one of the strongest is through fear of failure.

We hesitate to act because we're fearful of doing something wrong. Or we fear that our actions will deliver poor results. And importantly, it doesn't matter whether our presumed failure happens privately or publicly. Both are unpleasant outcomes, and many of us will go to great lengths to avoid them.

This fearfulness can stem from a number of things. For example, lack of familiarity with a given task or process may cause us to hesitate. The unfamiliarity makes the outcome of our actions more uncertain, which exacerbates our fear of failure. We end up deliberating whether it's necessary to act immediately or if the task in question can be delayed.

Our fear of failure may also be prompted by a past experience that was embarrassing or traumatic in some way. For example, suppose you once bombed while speaking in front of a large audience. The experience was embarrassing for you, enough so that it has become ingrained in your memory. Unless you've since participated in successful speaking engagements that mitigated the feelings behind that earlier traumatic experience, you might be disinclined to speak in front of an audience again. At the very least, you'd look for ways to delay doing so.

Fear of failure can also surface as the result of repeated indoctrination about a presumed inability to do something. For example, a child who's told over and over that she's a terrible student might grow to fear taking exams, and procrastinate studying for them. A salesperson who's frequently told that his sales approach is ineffective might put off cold calling new prospects.

Some people - I include myself in this camp - harbor a natural aversion to trying new things. This aversion, which often prompts feelings of anxiety, makes us reluctant to take action. In fact, some of us would delay taking action indefinitely if doing so was an option.

How To Overcome Fear Of Failure

First, realize that fear of failure is part of human nature. Our egos are entwined with our ability to succeed at whatever we pursue. The idea that we might fail is vexing to us.

Second, redefine the meaning of failure as it relates to your life. Rather than defining it as the result of a character flaw - e.g. you're destined to fail because you're imperfect - redefine it as simple feedback that a given action or tactic isn't working. Once you do so, you can come up with a different approach that has a greater chance of success. In other words, view failure as useful data rather than an indignity you're forced to endure.

Third, consider that some of the world's most successful people failed miserably at various points in their lives. Their failures didn't stop them from achieving greatness. On the contrary, failure propelled them forward, filling them with the desire to succeed.

For example, Abraham Lincoln lost numerous elections before finally becoming President of the United States. Film director Steven Spielberg was rejected by the University of Southern California three times due to poor grades. J.K Rowling, author the blockbuster Harry Potter series, claims she *"failed on an epic scale"* but her failures drove her to success.[1]

Along the same lines, basketball star Michael Jordan had this to say about his time in the NBA and how failure affected him:

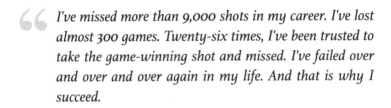

I've missed more than 9,000 shots in my career. I've lost almost 300 games. Twenty-six times, I've been trusted to take the game-winning shot and missed. I've failed over and over and over again in my life. And that is why I succeed.

To overcome fear of failure, think about the worst possible outcome. It's probably not as bad as you imagine. Then, redefine what failure means to you. Consider how you might leverage it - remember, it's just feedback - rather than letting it stop you from taking action.

---

1. https://www.ted.com/talks/jk_rowling_the_fringe_benefits_of_failure

FEAR OF SUCCESS

~

Fear of success can be just as debilitating as fear of failure. It stems from an innate worry about one's ability to live up to expectations - either personal expectations or those of other people. To that end, it causes many folks to postpone taking action.

For example, suppose your boss announces the launch of a new division of your company. He wants you to spearhead it. All you have to do is accept the offer.

You may initially be excited by the prospects of heading your own division. You'll enjoy more visibility, more autonomy, a promotion, and a healthy pay raise. But soon after, doubts surface, causing you to question your abilities.

Will you be able to lead the new division to success? Will you be able to meet your boss's expectations? What happens if you stumble, and the new division flails under your leadership?

These and other doubts, left unchallenged, can fester to the point that they paralyze you.

Fear of success can also stem from concerns about the challenges that success will bring. For example, suppose you turn your company's new division into a major contender in its industry. What will happen next?

Will your boss ask you to lead an even larger project, which will pose even greater challenges? Would taking on this hypothetical larger project set you up for potential failure? Will your continued and high-profile success cause you to lose your identity?

Sometimes, fear of success is borne from guilt. For example, you might believe that your past successes were due to factors outside your control. Consequently, you feel undeserving of recognition and the opportunities your past successes have afforded you. You feel like an imposter.

Like fear of failure, fear of success is an act of self-sabotage. Regardless of what sets it off, the result is the same: the individual procrastinates.

How To Overcome Fear Of Success

The challenge with conquering this fear is that it's easy to miss. We often mistake fear of success as simple procrastination instead of investigating it as a *cause* of our procrastination.

First, look for signs that you're delaying taking action because you're fearful of success. Ask yourself whether receiving recognition concerns you. Are you worried that others might see you as a fraud? Are you nervous that you may not deliver as expected?

Second, ask yourself what might happen in the event you succeed. You'll nearly always find that your greatest fears are unfounded. Remember, fear, in all of its manifestations, is powerful because it hides from view. When we confront it head on, it contracts.

Third, ask yourself whether the outcome of success is consistent with your goals. Using our earlier example, suppose your company's new division becomes a major success under your capable direction. Will your success help you to achieve what you consider important in your life (e.g. a larger salary, more visibility, etc.)? If so, you can look forward to meeting these objectives by taking action. If not, your success will have minimal impact, and thus shouldn't be a concern.

Either way, this exercise will reveal that your presumed success shouldn't cause you to be fearful at all.

Confronting the fear that's causing you to procrastinate is the most effective way to disarm it. As with confronting fear of failure, you'll find that your fear of success is largely unfounded.

PERFECTIONISM

~

I'm a reformed perfectionist. So I can empathize if you're the type of person who is constantly paralyzed by self-imposed expectations.

Perfectionism is a common cause of procrastination. Perfectionists hold themselves to ultra-high standards and won't accept anything less. The upside of this trait is that it can spur an individual to produce work of amazing quality and startling depth. The downside is that it can prevent him or her from moving forward in the first place.

I grew up as a perfectionist. Everything I produced had to be flawless. This character quirk, which manifested in me as a child, persisted as I entered high school, and then college. It followed me as I entered Corporate America, and later as I left the corporate world to build my business.

How did it affect me? First, it completely skewed my perspective on what constituted acceptable work.

Second, I became habitually inclined to procrastinate whenever I had the slightest feeling that I would be unable to turn in flawless work.

Third, the more I put things off due to my perfectionist tendencies, the unhappier I became. Procrastination led to increased stress and frustration. In the end, my perfectionism was a compulsion that caused me to delay taking action on nearly every project. That, in turn, ultimately made me miserable.

Can you relate to this? Do you recognize some of what I've described in your own process? If so, you know firsthand how procrastination can be a symptom of perfectionism.

How To Overcome Perfectionism

First, identify the difference in reward between delivering something that's perfect and delivering something that's *nearly* perfect, but flawed in some minor way. You'll usually find that the difference is tiny - perhaps so tiny as to be unnoticeable. And if it's unnoticeable, it's hardly worth fretting over.

Second, consider the costs of being a perfectionist. Think of the many ways in which perfectionism is a liability. For example, it paralyzes you into a state of inaction; it increases your stress level; and it causes you to miss potentially rewarding opportunities.

Third, question *why* you want to be perfect. In most cases, you'll find there's no justifiable reason. Rather, there's an intrinsic fear of being unable to meet expectations, even when those expectations are unrealistic.

Lastly, realize that your efforts can deliver value even if your work is imperfect. For example, scoring a 95% on an exam may be less appealing than receiving a perfect score, but it's better than scoring a 70% or 80%. Mowing your lawn once a week has value even if your hedges aren't perfectly trimmed. An evening out with your spouse doesn't have to go perfectly for the two of you to fully enjoy each other's company.

Your inner perfectionist is a tyrant that adds little value to your life. Or as the acclaimed novelist Anne Lamott once said, *"perfectionism is the voice of the oppressor."* Quiet that voice and you'll be less inclined to procrastinate.

A FEELING OF OVERWHELM

~

There's no shame in feeling overwhelmed. It happens to all of us. Our obligations and responsibilities accumulate to the point that we feel buried underneath them. Anxiety sets in, paralyzing us and preventing us from taking action.

Many circumstances can lead to a general sense of overwhelm. The most common example is that of the harried individual juggling multiple projects. The demands of each eventually cause him or her to feel as if they're facing an insurmountable mountain.

But that's just the most common scenario. In truth, the feeling of overwhelm can stem from many situations.

For example, relationship problems between you and your spouse can trigger anxiety that paralyzes you into inaction. Massive credit card balances can have the same effect. The death of a close family member can make everything else seem doubly stressful and oppressive. Major life decisions, such as buying a new house, can dramatically elevate your stress level, opening the door to a host of negative emotions.

Information overload can also make us feel overwhelmed. While researching something, we're inundated with so much information that it's difficult to move forward. We become incapacitated with indecision.

Whatever the cause, feeling overwhelmed increases the likelihood that we'll put off work, oftentimes *important* work. The sense of being buried paralyzes us, making it difficult to act - at least until this feeling, along with the negative emotions it spurs, dissipates.

How To Overcome A Feeling Of Overwhelm

If you're feeling overwhelmed, and that feeling is causing you to put things off, take a step back and figure out the reason (or reasons). Why are you feeling this way? What precisely is causing you to feel overwhelmed? Only then can you create a plan for tackling the triggers and resolving the feelings that are holding you back.

For example, suppose you're feeling overwhelmed because you're not getting enough sleep. Your nerves are frayed, you're irritable, and minor annoyances are magnified. In this case, insufficient sleep is the trigger. You'd need to come up with a plan for getting the sleep your mind needs to perform effectively.

Suppose you're feeling stressed because you're juggling multiple projects. Fragmented focus is the trigger. Here, it's helpful to break down each project into its constituent tasks. Then, address each task one by one.

Suppose you're feeling overwhelmed because a loved one has died. In this case, therapy might prove invaluable.

If credit card bills are causing you to feel anxious and trapped, it's imperative that you come up with a *reasonable* plan for paying them off.

There's no one-size-fits-all solution for dealing with a feeling of overwhelm. The most effective method for controlling this feeling is to identify its root cause and address it at its source.

LAZINESS

~

Many people think laziness and procrastination are so closely entwined that they're essentially the same thing. In truth, they're entirely different behavioral aspects. While laziness often leads to procrastination, many chronic procrastinators aren't lazy at all.

Let's unpack this concept with a couple of definitions:

- Laziness is an unwillingness to perform a task.
- Procrastination is delaying taking action on a task.

Notice the difference?

The procrastinator realizes that the task in question must eventually be addressed. He or she simply puts it off until a later time.

A good example is studying for an exam. The procrastinating student knows that he or she must eventually sit down and study for it. The exam isn't going to go away.

The *lazy* student doesn't just put off studying. He or she avoids it entirely. There's no intention of addressing the task in question - neither in the present nor down the road. It entails effort, which the lazy person finds objectionable.

Let's say you struggle with laziness, and habitually put tasks off until the last possible moment. Or worse, you put them off indefinitely. You know you should address important items that appear on your to-do list, but would rather sit on the couch and watch TV.

How can you break this habit?

How To Overcome Laziness

First, identify the reasons you tend to be lazy. Some people are lazy because they harbor a low self-image. Others are so because they have absolutely no interest in the task at hand. Still others use laziness as a coping mechanism when they're faced with a task they find disagreeable.

Although laziness is considered by many to be a natural character trait, there's usually a root cause that triggers the behavior. The key, as always, is to identify that trigger.

Second, identify obstacles you believe are preventing you from taking action. Ask yourself whether these obstacles are truly impossible to overcome. When you scrutinize them, you may find they're little more than mirages. They either don't exist, or they're far less impactful than you imagine. They may even be invented as a way to rationalize behavior.

For example, suppose you're trying to motivate yourself to go for a jog. A possible "obstacle" might be that you don't know where you left your running shoes. But this isn't likely to be a *true* obstacle. After all, there are only so many places your running shoes could be located in your home. In this example, the "obstacle" has been invented to rationalize laziness.

Third, get into the habit of taking action. Most people who

struggle with laziness believe the issue stems from a lack of motivation. In truth, motivation is fleeting for *everyone*. What separates the action taker from the excuse maker is the *habit* of acting.

The good news is that this habit, like all habits, can be learned. The key ingredients are time and consistent application.

BOREDOM

~

A few days ago, I sat down to write a blog post. You'd think I'd be disciplined enough to focus and knock it out in record time.

But I'm ashamed to say that's not what happened at all.

Instead, I found myself reading other blogs, visiting a forum that I frequent, and checking the performance of my advertising campaigns. In other words, I was doing everything *but* writing the blog post.

It took me a few minutes to figure out the reason: I was bored. This boredom meant that my heart wasn't really into writing the blog post. So I did what most people do when confronted by a task they'd rather avoid...

I procrastinated.

With a little soul-searching, I eventually uncovered the reason I was bored. It turned out the topic of the blog post held absolutely no interest for me. So, rather than fighting against my boredom to write about the topic, I discarded it and chose another - one that excited me.

You can probably guess what happened. My fingers flew across the keyboard. I was focused and taking action.

Why the sudden change in behavior? Because the new topic was interesting to me. That made it easy to overcome my procrastination. In fact, I didn't consciously seek that outcome. I simply started writing, and my brain did the rest.

Whenever you find yourself procrastinating, ask yourself whether you're bored with the task at hand. If you *are* bored, figure out a way to kill your boredom, removing the mental roadblocks to taking action.

How To Overcome Boredom

Boredom with a task can stem from a few different causes. For example, your heart may not be into it (similar to my personal example above). Or maybe you're working on a repetitive task you're so familiar with that you could do in your sleep. Or perhaps your boredom is due to not knowing why the task is important.

The approach you take in conquering your boredom will depend on the reason you're feeling bored.

If your heart's not into a task, try to change things in a way that stimulates your mind. Be creative. For example, come up with a way to perform the task so that it requires you to use multiple skills. Or involve other people in its completion.

If you're working on a repetitive task, create a little game that makes performing it fun. For example, how many envelopes can you stuff in 20 minutes without making a single mistake? If your coworkers are doing the same task, turn it into a friendly competition.

If you're not sure why the task at hand is important, ask your boss for clarification. If you don't have a boss - for example, you're a freelancer, stay-at-home parent, or college student - determine whether the task needs to be addressed at all.

Boredom is self-imposed. We control the triggers that make us feel bored. That means we can develop tailored strategies to help us conquer our boredom, and thereby overcome our impulse to procrastinate.

AVERSION TO HARD WORK

~

Most of us are averse to hard work unless our effort results in a speedy payoff. For example, we're willing to wash our vehicles because they look nice immediately afterward. We study for looming exams to achieve good grades. We clean out our email inboxes because a clean inbox is immediately gratifying.

By contrast, it's difficult to get motivated to exercise. Why? Because the results only become evident weeks, or even months, in the future. Likewise, it's difficult to put in the hours needed to build a side business. Why? Because it can take years for that business to become a success.

I'm sure you can relate to this. Everyone can.

A non-critical task that requires a lot of effort is likely to be postponed if it doesn't deliver quick gratification. It's so much easier to take the path of least (or lesser) resistance. That might entail watching TV, hanging out with friends, or addressing tasks that require less effort.

The problem is, putting off tasks because they require too

much effort sets the stage for future stress and guilt as the postponed tasks pile up. That being the case, it's important to overcome this innate resistance to hard work.

How To Overcome An Aversion To Hard Work

The most effective strategy I've found for taking action on difficult tasks is to have a system in place. Having a system means I never need to rely on motivation or willpower. My actions are instead dictated by habits that complement my preplanned schedule and to-do lists.

If you regularly procrastinate because you're averse to hard work, I strongly recommend that you try the following approach.

Suppose you'd like to create a side business to generate extra income. Building any type of business is hard work. It requires a lot of hours and attention. And the payoff is often delayed until months, even years, down the road.

If you think of creating a side business in those dismal terms, you'll face a lot of internal resistance. Your mind will try to convince you to put off tasks integral to building the business, and instead focus on things that promise to be more fun and immediately gratifying.

You can overcome this resistance by creating a *system*. For example, you might commit to working on your side business from 6:00 p.m. to 7:00 p.m each evening. Doing so over the course of a few weeks turns the practice into a habit. You end up working on your business each day during that time block, regardless of whether you're motivated.

Or you might identify three tasks that are essential to getting your fledgling business off the ground, and commit to addressing them each morning, immediately after waking.

When you follow a *system*, you're no longer focused on the mammoth amount of time and effort involved with achieving your end goal. Instead, you're only focused on what you should be doing that day. Meanwhile, and importantly, you're developing the habit of taking action on a daily basis.

Assuming you're addressing the right tasks, your daily effort should ultimately produce your desired results - in our example, a business that generates a side income.

NEGATIVE SELF-TALK

~

N egative self-talk, or *self-downing*, is the act of belittling yourself in your own mind. You disparage your abilities and skills. In extreme cases, this can occur to the extent that you begin to doubt your ability to do anything at all. You lose faith in yourself.

Negative self-talk is an act of self-sabotage. It allows your inner critic - all of us have one - to ride roughshod over your self-confidence. Worse, the negative murmurings of your inner critic are usually wrong. At the very least, they're overly-critical and deserve to be challenged.

The alternative is to give your inner critic free rein over your thinking. This will almost certainly lead to procrastination as you become filled with self-doubt. The self-downing will make you feel as if you're destined to fail. Consequently, you'll hesitate to take action because you distrust your ability to do so effectively.

For example, suppose you're considering seeking an advanced degree in your field of specialty. But your inner critic whispers that you'll probably fail because there's too much work involved.

If you allow this negative self-talk to persist without challenge, you may be inclined to procrastinate enrolling into your preferred graduate program. Put off doing so for too long, and you might completely miss out on the opportunity.

Fortunately, you don't have to be your inner critic's punching bag. You can silence the negative self-talk, get rid of the self-doubt, and get into the habit of taking action with confidence.

How To Overcome Negative Self-Talk

The first step toward silencing your inner critic is to challenge his or her every assertion. If he or she whispers, "You're going to fail," immediately dispute the claim. Ask yourself why you're destined to fail. What factors will supposedly contribute to your failure? What circumstances are going to make success impossible?

In other words, what *evidence* supports the assertion?

Shining a bright investigative light on negative self-talk causes it to evaporate. It's unable to withstand scrutiny.

The second step is to seek perspective on the situation. Let's use our earlier example of seeking an advanced degree in your field. Your inner critic says you'll fail to follow through because obtaining the degree entails too much work.

But is this claim actually true?

You probably have a firm grasp on the amount of work involved with obtaining the degree. After all, you've completed your undergraduate studies. You know what to expect, and are prepared for it. As long as you're willing to put in the necessary time and effort, you're almost sure to succeed, regardless of what your inner critic claims.

The third step is to learn to accept compliments. Most people burdened with negative self-talk become uncomfortable when others praise them. Their discomfort arises from the fact that others' praise conflicts with how they view themselves.

If you have difficulty accepting compliments, I urge you to make an effort to become comfortable with them. Others' praise can help to "rewire" your self-perception. When someone compliments you, simply say "Thank you." You may be surprised by how effective this simple practice is in quieting your inner critic.

With your inner critic silenced, you'll be less likely to put things off and more inclined to act with confidence in your skills and abilities.

LOW TOLERANCE FOR ADVERSE EVENTS

~

Do you quickly become frustrated when things don't go as planned? Are you prone to anger or despair when circumstances don't go your way? If so, these feelings might be related to low frustration tolerance, or LFT.

Low frustration tolerance is a mindset that perceives adverse events as being far worse than they truly are.

For example, suppose you're driving to your office, are running behind schedule, and are stopped by a red traffic light. Most people might say to themselves, "Darn. Just my luck. Oh well."

By contrast, someone who struggles with LFT might say to themselves, "This is terrible! I'm already behind schedule, and this red light makes it worse. My morning is ruined!"

A person who's unable to tolerate adverse events will instinctively try to avoid any situation that might lead to a less-than-ideal outcome. Tasks become "too hard." Responsibilities become "unfair." Projects become "undoable."

The end result is procrastination. Tasks are postponed;

responsibilities are shirked; and projects are avoided. The individual becomes paralyzed with inaction since the alternative (taking action) carries the ever-present potential for adversity and distress.

How To Overcome A Low Tolerance For Adverse Events

I used to have this type of mindset. Small problems bothered me a great deal, often to the point that I couldn't focus on anything else. It was an irrational way of thinking, and almost always led to my putting things off.

I was eventually able to resolve this issue with the help of several tactics. Here's a brief rundown of them:

First, I came to realize that my intolerance for distress was mostly in my mind. That is, my agitation when things didn't go my way wasn't due to external stimuli. It was due to the way I *internalized* those stimuli.

For example, having to wait 30 minutes for a table at my favorite restaurant wasn't causing my distress. My impatience was causing it.

Second, I developed the habit of grading each adverse event on a scale ranging from one to 10. One meant an event was harmless. Ten meant it was worthy of DEFCON 1. By grading events, I was able to put each one in perspective.

For example, hitting a red traffic light, while inconvenient, was far less severe than having my car totaled in a traffic accident. As such, it warranted a far lesser reaction. Rating the red traffic light accordingly gave me a more practical outlook.

Third, I looked for opportunities to desensitize myself to adverse circumstances. By doing so, I became less inclined to lose my cool when things didn't go my way.

For example, I'd visit my favorite restaurant during times I knew it would be crowded. This forced me to wait for a table.

Ultimately, doing so forced me to come to terms with my impatience.

These measures gradually made me more tolerant of circumstances that got in the way of immediate gratification. As a result, I became less inclined to put things off and better able to handle the frustration of things going differently than planned.

To be clear, I wouldn't describe myself as a stoic. But I'm no longer fearful of the distress and discomfort posed by adverse events.

If you struggle with low frustration tolerance, I encourage you to try the three steps I've described above. You may find they radically change the way you perceive everything that happens around you.

UNCERTAINTY ABOUT HOW (OR WHERE) TO START

~

Does the following scenario sounds familiar?

You have a mountain of work in front of you. Your to-do list is so long that you know you'll never be able to complete every task on it. Meanwhile, the time you have available to work is ticking away.

You're overwhelmed. You have too much on your plate. As a result, you don't know where to start.

So you procrastinate. It's easier to check your email than to address the mountain of work in front of you.

Here's another common scenario.

You're responsible for completing an important project. Its outcome will have a ripple effect on your career or social status (or both). That being the case, you want to take the best possible course of action.

The problem is, you're not sure what that course of action is. So you procrastinate. It's easier to check Facebook than it is to decide how to start your project, especially given its import.

Here's another scenario that may strike a familiar chord.

You need to complete an important task, but lack the necessary information to do so. Perhaps you know how to obtain the information you need, but the process of doing so is unappealing to you (e.g. you must seek help from someone you dislike). Or maybe you don't know how to obtain the information at all.

Either way, you're stuck.

So you procrastinate. It's easier to scan the latest news headlines than to deal with this challenge.

Uncertainty regarding how to start on a task or project makes us more susceptible to distractions. Unless we've trained ourselves to act otherwise, we'll follow our natural impulse: we'll avoid the problem, and instead pursue activities that allow us to defer taking action. Some might even deliver immediate gratification, which makes them doubly appealing. Such activities might include reading email, checking Facebook, scanning news headlines, playing video games, or watching Youtube videos.

Do you often find yourself struggling with the above scenarios? If so, here are my recommendations for beating this problem.

How To Overcome Uncertainty About How (Or Where) To Start

If you're paralyzed by a mountain of work, the best thing you can do is simply start. Pick a task and address it, ignoring everything else on your plate.

It doesn't matter which task you choose. The important thing is that you take action. You'll find that you'll gain momentum once you get started. Working on the first task will carry you into the second one, and then the next one, and so on.

If you're procrastinating because you don't know the best course of action to take on a project, reevaluate the potential outcomes associated with different approaches. There's a good chance you're envisioning a potential catastrophe when the likely outcome of a particular approach is far less serious.

This type of procrastination is related to fear of failure. We fear the worst, even if such an outcome is improbable. This fear paralyzes us and prompts our brains to seek distractions. The important thing to realize is that the fear is irrational. Scrutinizing it will cause it to evaporate.

If you lack information necessary to completing a task or project, figure out the simplest way to obtain it. Then, pursue that option even if it poses challenges. For example, if obtaining the information requires you to seek help from someone you dislike, accept that doing so is necessary. Grin and bear it. If possible, use it as an opportunity to extend an olive branch to that individual.

Apprehension regarding how or where to start is a state of fear that we impose upon ourselves. That's good news because it means we're ultimately in control. Taking action banishes doubts, and replaces them with self-confidence. It also prevents the brain from seeking distractions as a way to avoid the distress borne of uncertainty.

INABILITY TO MAKE DECISIONS

~

I ndecision is the arch nemesis of our ability to take action. It paralyzes us and makes it impossible to move forward. Tasks and projects are put off until we manage to break out of the deliberation loop.

Nearly every action we take is preceded by a choice between two or more options. When we come to these cognitive forks in the road, we contemplate the options in front of us before moving forward. This is a natural and beneficial process. It helps us to select the options that best compliment our goals and circumstances.

But some folks get caught in a deliberation loop. They get stuck at the contemplation stage. They never manage to choose between the options in front of them. Their indecisiveness invariably causes them to delay taking action. In extreme cases, in the absence of a sufficiently-compelling incentive to act - for example, a boss threatening termination - the delay becomes perpetual.

Indecisiveness can stem from many factors, some of which we've already explored.

For example, an individual may be worried that choosing an inferior option will cause him or her to be unsuccessful (fear of failure). He may be concerned that choosing poorly will force him to produce imperfect work (perfectionism). She might fear that making the wrong selection will generate unappealing results (aversion to risk).

Whatever its cause, indecisiveness always makes us more prone to procrastination. We're more likely to delay taking action until we're certain that we're making the right choices. This predicament, of course, can persist indefinitely.

I speak from experience. I used to have great difficulty choosing between multiple options. Here are a couple of simple tactics I used to overcome this problem.

How To Overcome An Inability To Make Decisions

The most important step you can take to overcome indecisiveness is to *decide* to make a decision. That is, commit to taking action, even if doing so means inadvertently choosing the lesser of two or more options.

Taking action short-circuits our impulse to procrastinate as we wait for additional details to make better decisions. This is good because we rarely *need* more details. In most cases, we simply convince ourselves that we do in order to postpone making a choice between competing options. It's our way of dealing with fear and discomfort about the unknown.

The important thing to remember is that this fear and discomfort are rarely warranted. The true cost of choosing a less-than-ideal option is usually negligible. Meanwhile, the cost of allowing fear and discomfort to rob us of our ability to make decisions is significant; it sabotages our productivity.

In addition to making a commitment to take action in the face of uncertainty, it's important to grow comfortable with making imperfect decisions. This is a practice I used to great effect in conquering my own indecisiveness. I developed the habit of asking myself, "What's the worst that can happen if I choose the wrong option?" In most cases, the worst-case scenario wasn't bad at all. At most, it was simply less positive than choosing the ideal option.

For example, I would agonize over choosing a restaurant to host a get-together with friends. Should we meet at a Mexican restaurant? A Chinese restaurant? A gourmet burger joint? I would overthink the decision, and become paralyzed in the process. Naturally, I'd procrastinate the decision, often to the point that it became impossible to make a reservation.

Ultimately, the choice didn't matter. The worst-case scenario was that we'd endure bad service or imperfect food. But that was a risk with *all* of restaurants. In the end, the only thing that truly mattered was that everyone in our group enjoyed each other's company. We would have done so regardless of the venue.

Here's the takeaway: if you struggle with indecisiveness, get into the habit of taking action. Put an end to the deliberation stage. You'll find that whichever option you choose, the outcome won't be nearly as bad as you might imagine.

OPTIONS THAT PROMISE MORE
IMMEDIATE GRATIFICATION

~

Given the choice between receiving a benefit in the present and receiving it in the future, and assuming all other variables are the same, all of us would choose the former. There would be no compelling reason to delay gratification.

For example, if someone offered to give us $100 today or $100 a year from today, we'd want to receive it today.

Of course, life is rarely that simple.

In many cases, choosing immediate gratification means receiving a smaller reward in the present in lieu of a bigger payoff later. For example, suppose you spend $1,000 on a shopping spree. Doing so offers instant satisfaction. But had you invested that $1,000, it might have grown exponentially over your lifetime, providing a much larger payoff in retirement.

Sometimes, choosing short-term satisfaction means sabotaging future goals. For example, suppose you'd like to lose weight, and have thus decided to forgo unhealthy foods.

Suddenly, you're tempted to eat a delectable donut. Giving in to this temptation would deliver immediate rewards: appealing taste, sugar high, dopamine rush, etc. But doing so would also sabotage your long-term goal: weight loss.

For many of us, pursuing immediate gratification is a task-avoidance measure. Our decision isn't motivated exclusively by the rewards we expect to receive in the present. Rather, we make the decision, in part, because doing so allows us to delay taking action on something else.

For example, suppose you intend to mow your lawn. Because you dread the task, your mind will look for ways to postpone it. To this end, you may be tempted to watch television rather than address your lawn.

Here, you're not motivated by your favorite shows. Your shows may not even be scheduled for broadcast at the time you're making the decision. Instead, the *true* reward is being able to avoid the task at hand.

Think of the many ways we chase present comfort as a way to avoid tasks and projects we should be working on. We check Facebook, watch YouTube videos, read blogs, check email, buy things on Amazon, and text our friends.

These distractions aren't the problem. The *true* problem is our tendency to use them as a way to procrastinate.

How To Forgo Short-Term Gratification

Instant gratification is like a drug. Once you experience it, you want to relive the experience again and again. Over time, it's easy to develop a habit that becomes an addiction.

You may be able to relate to this firsthand. If you constantly find yourself putting off tasks in favor of activities that deliver immediate satisfaction, the habit has likely become ingrained in your mind. Making such decisions might even be instinctive.

Here are a few tips for breaking the habit, learning to forgo present comfort in favor of taking action on the work in front of you.

First, consider the consequences of procrastinating. Will doing so cause you to turn in shoddy work? Will it cause you to miss deadlines? Will putting things off increase your stress levels and lead to a feeling of overwhelm as tasks pile up?

It's easier to justify our procrastination when we ignore its long-term consequences. Shining a bright, investigative light on these consequences erodes that justification.

Second, practice impulse control. Our tendency to pursue immediate satisfaction is related to our ability to resist our urges. These urges can be so compelling that they're nearly impossible to resist.

The good news is that we can learn to control our impulses. The key is to start slowly and build discipline over time.

For example, if you normally procrastinate by checking social media, use a website blocker (e.g. SelfControl, Freedom, HeyFocus, etc.) to block Facebook and Twitter for 30 minutes at a time. Gradually increase the duration of the blocks each week.

A third tactic is to interrupt your urges at their source. For example, get rid of the social media apps on your phone. Remove bookmarks to your favorite time-wasting websites from your browser (being forced to type URLs manually may dissuade you from visiting the sites). If you normally watch television as a task-avoidance measure, put the remote control somewhere that requires effort to retrieve it (for example, on a rafter in your garage).

Fourth, create a reward system. Reward yourself whenever you successfully delay gratification and take action.

A friend of mine uses a points system. He awards himself points for each success and deducts points for each failure. When he accumulates a certain number of points, he permits himself a desired reward - for example, buying a new CD or attending a concert.

Learning to delay gratification will make you less prone to procrastination. This skill will not only give you greater control over your impulses, but will also increase your productivity and lessen your stress.

NO IMMEDIATE CONSEQUENCES FOR INACTION

~

Think back to your childhood when your parents told you to clean your room. If you disregarded their demand, you could expect consequences. For example, you wouldn't get to go outside and play with your friends. You wouldn't get to watch television. You wouldn't get to play your favorite video games.

With these consequences looming over you like a dark cloud, you cleaned your room. The promised repercussions for inaction spurred you to take action.

This is an important lesson to consider. Many of us procrastinate today because there are rarely immediate consequences for doing so. Our parents and teachers no longer hover over our shoulders. Our bosses provide instructions, set deadlines, and then leave us to our own devices.

While the autonomy is appealing, it's also dangerous, particularly for the habitual procrastinator. Without the risk of immediate consequences, he or she is likely to put off tasks and projects in favor of activities that deliver satisfaction in the present.

For example, suppose your boss tasks you with giving a presentation to your department next week. Nothing bad will happen tomorrow if you put off preparing for it. Nor will anything bad happen the following day, or the day after that. After all, you have an entire week. Given the absence of immediate repercussions for inaction, you may be tempted to waste time surfing the internet, reading news articles, and watching YouTube videos.

In other words, without the threat of swift consequences, you're likely to procrastinate.

The irony is that procrastination always imposes costs, many of which can be significant. We addressed many of them in the section *The Personal And Professional Price Of Procrastination*. So any justification to defer action based on the absence of consequences is misguided and shortsighted. Habitual inaction can have a profoundly negative impact on your personal life and career.

I learned this lesson the hard way. In fact, I had to learn it over and over before it finally sunk in. When I was a chronic procrastinator, I routinely put things off because the consequences for doing so were never immediate. I'd thus convince myself that the cost of procrastinating was minimal.

This "theory" turned out to be completely untrue. My life, career, and side businesses suffered for my ignorance.

To end on a positive, encouraging note, I'm no longer a chronic procrastinator. I've managed to tame that beast. And I'm going to show you exactly how I did it in *Part II: 21 Ways To Beat Your Inner Procrastinator*.

Before we move on to *Part II*, let's take a quick quiz to gauge your tendency to procrastinate.

POP QUIZ: ARE YOU A HABITUAL PROCRASTINATOR?

~

Everyone procrastinates from time to time. The question is, how likely are you to do it in any given situation? And do you procrastinate to the point that your inaction has an measurably negative impact on your life?

Some people know they're chronic procrastinators and openly admit as much. They recognize the problem.

Others regularly procrastinate, but have convinced themselves that their inaction isn't a problem or it's beyond their control. They either hoodwink themselves regarding how often they do it or regarding their ability to overcome the temptation.

Below, we're going to assess your procrastination habit. Rate the following 15 statements from one to five. An answer of "one" means the statement does not describe you. "Five" means it's highly accurate.

After you've rated the 15 statements from one to five, we'll tally your score to gauge your tendency to put things off.

1. I often find myself racing against the clock to complete tasks on time.
2. I regularly miscalculate the amount of time that tasks will take to complete.
3. I often put tasks off until the following day.
4. When faced with an unappealing task, I look for something more engaging to work on.
5. I often address tasks days after they were scheduled.
6. When I'm tasked with projects that have long-term deadlines, I wait until the last minute to start working on them.
7. I often catch myself daydreaming when I should be working.
8. When faced with a difficult task, I'm easily distracted by social media, texts, email, etc.
9. I'm often late to meetings, appointments, and social functions.
10. My workspace is in a constant state of disarray.
11. I never get through my daily to-do lists.
12. My email inbox and voicemail inbox are filled with unanswered messages.
13. I often pay bills late.
14. My favorite phrase is "I'll do it tomorrow."
15. You've abandoned this quiz at least once to do something else.

Did you rate each of the 15 statements from one to five? If so, it's time to find out how big a procrastinator you truly are.

Are You A Habitual Procrastinator?

Let's tally up your points.

. . .

15 TO 30 points - you don't have a problem with procrastination. You might occasionally put things off - all of us do so now and then - but you typically roll up your sleeves and proactively work on tasks.

31 TO 45 points - You're somewhat of a procrastinator. There are likely select areas of your life that suffer from your tendency to put things off. But you normally take action before your workload overwhelms you.

46 TO 60 points - Procrastination is a part of your daily life. You're easily distracted, particularly when confronted by difficult or unappealing tasks. You regularly procrastinate to avoid such tasks. You often work on projects right before they're due, and as a result, sometimes miss deadlines.

61 TO 75 points - You're the perfect example of a habitual procrastinator. You regularly arrive late to appointments and meetings, and do so unprepared. You typically start working on tasks at the last possible minute. You constantly miss deadlines despite working frantically to meet them. Your stress level is continually elevated as postponed tasks threaten to overwhelm you.

IF YOU SCORED 30 points or fewer, you probably don't need this book. Unless you're reading it as a way to avoid some other task. In that case, stick with me.

If you scored between 31 and 60 points, you'll definitely find value in *The Procrastination Cure*. The tactics I'll share with you in *Part II: 21 Ways To Beat Your Inner Procrastinator* will pay for themselves over and over throughout your life.

If you scored more than 60 points, we have our work cut out for us. The procrastination habit is deeply rooted in your psyche. That means you're going to face a lot of internal resistance as you try to curb the habit. But with grit and resolve, success is not only possible, it's to be expected.

Coming Up Next

You're now aware of the reasons you procrastinate. You also know the extent to which procrastination negatively impacts your life.

In *Part II: 21 Ways To Beat Your Inner Procrastinator*, I'll give you a veritable treasure trove of tactics you can use to overcome this habit.

Let's dig in...

PART II

21 WAYS TO BEAT YOUR INNER PROCRASTINATOR

~

This section of *The Procrastination Cure* is chock-full of operational tactics that'll help you to overcome your tendency to put things off. These are the measures I used to conquer my own inner procrastinator, and I'm 100% confident they'll work for you, as well.

You may be tempted to breeze through them without any intention of applying them. Don't do that. I strongly encourage you to read through them carefully, one by one, in the order they appear. After each one, take a few moments to consider how you'll apply the practice in your daily process. Visualize putting it in action every day, and imagine how doing so will help curb your procrastination habit.

Each of the tactics that appear in *The Procrastination Cure* can be implemented immediately and easily. Once you've read through this section, implement one tactic each week.

Don't rush. Give yourself time to make each one a habit. By

the time you apply all of these tactics, your inner procrastinator will seem like a past acquaintance with whom you have no desire to reconnect.

Let's roll up our sleeves and get to work.

TACTIC #1: EAT THE FROG FIRST

~

Imagine starting the day with a to-do list that includes a task you're absolutely dreading. It's one of those awful tasks you'd prefer to put off until you have no choice but to address it.

For example, I've always hated doing laundry. I used to put it off until my closet looked bare, and my hampers had started to overflow. There were times when doing a load of laundry was the only way I'd have something clean to wear outside my home.

To curb this habit, I learned to do my laundry first thing in the morning. It felt great to cross the task off my to-do list. I also found that everything else on my list was easier - or at least more pleasant - by comparison.

American writer and humorist Mark Twain called this practice "eating the frog" first. Here's the full quote:

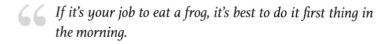 *If it's your job to eat a frog, it's best to do it first thing in the morning.*

Twain called unappealing tasks "frogs." These are the tasks and projects for which you have no motivation. They hang over you like a dark cloud until you address them. The longer you put them off, the more stress they cause you to feel.

It's natural to put these "frogs" on the back burner, addressing them at the end of your day. But that's the worst thing you can do. Not only will they loom and cause you stress, but you'll have less energy to deal with them. That'll only make them more difficult to work on, and easier to postpone until the following day.

Tackle your "frog" as early as possible. Get it out of the way. You may be surprised by how exhilarating doing so can make you feel. It'll give you a sense of accomplishment. You'll also find that the rest of your day is easier by comparison.

What if your to-do list contains more than one dreadful task? I recommend following Twain's advice:

> *If it's your job to eat two frogs, it's best to eat the biggest one first.*

One of your "frogs" will be less appealing than the other. Address that one first. Then, address the second one immediately afterward.

For example, I dislike cleaning the bathrooms in my home nearly as much as I dread doing laundry. The important distinction is "nearly as much." So if both tasks are on my to-do list, I'll tackle the laundry first.

TACTIC #2: DO THE FIRST 10 MINUTES

~

Tasks often seem more daunting than they truly are. But in most cases, the difficulty they seem to impose is just a mirage. It's a figment of our imaginations.

I've found that the biggest challenge isn't *completing* seemingly-daunting tasks. It's *starting* them. Once we start doing something, even something we dread, working on that task becomes easier.

For example, suppose you intend to visit the gym for a vigorous workout. The problem is, you're not motivated to do so. Finding your workout clothes, driving to the gym, working out, and driving home, is likely to take an hour or longer. In that light, it's a daunting - and even unappealing - endeavor.

So you tell yourself that you'll visit the gym tomorrow.

But if you were to simply get started - for example, find your workout clothes and drive to the gym - you'd find it much easier to continue. You'd build momentum. When you arrive at the gym, it's almost a certainty that you'd work out.

Whenever you're thinking about putting off a task, don't think of it on a macro level. Instead, focus on the first few steps. Focus on the first 10 minutes.

For example, if you're postponing mowing the lawn, don't think about the hour it will take. Instead, focus on getting the lawn mower out of your garage and pushing it that first step.

If you're procrastinating on preparing a presentation for your boss, don't think about the presentation in its entirety. Instead, focus on opening the appropriate software on your computer and collecting the resources you need to proceed.

If you're putting off decluttering your office, don't think about making it completely clutter-free. Instead, focus on decluttering a single corner of your workspace.

In other words, do the first 10 minutes. Once you get started, you'll find it much easier to continue.

I use this tactic whenever I start to write a new book, or even a new chapter in a book. I find the blank page to be daunting. It's like facing a tall mountain and planning to climb its shear cliffs.

In that light, it's difficult to start writing. But I've found that if I write for 10 minutes, continuing to do so is easy and effortless.

Don't take my word for it. I encourage you to try this tactic for yourself. The next time you find yourself procrastinating on a big task, focus on taking the first step toward completing it. Work on it for 10 minutes. I'll bet you'll find that completing it, or at least continuing to work on it, is easier than you had imagined.

TACTIC #3: REWARD YOURSELF

~

We procrastinate on tasks that are unappealing to us. We're hardwired to do so when other options offer more - or more immediate - gratification.

For example, we choose to go out with our friends instead of studying for an upcoming exam. We watch TV instead of washing our vehicles. We go shopping instead of visiting the gym.

But what if you could enjoy the fun activities while still completing everything on your to-do list? You can! It's just a matter of setting up a smart reward system.

Rewards have a huge influence on our behaviors. They can prompt us to take action, help us to form good habits, and spur us to perform at levels we can be proud of. The key is to come up with a system that keeps you on track throughout the day.

There are lots of ways to do this, and it's important to find the way that works best for you. In the section *Options That Promise More Immediate Gratification*, I mentioned my friend's points system. He accrues or subtracts points from a total based on his actions. The points he accrues permit him to spend money on things he enjoys, such as new CDs or concert tickets. It's a creative way to use rewards as leverage. It works well for him.

Another strategy is to set up your day so that each unappealing task is followed by an activity you enjoy. The trick is to match each rewarding activity to a correspondingly off-putting task.

For example, suppose you have the following to-do list:

- Clean the bathrooms
- Visit the grocery store
- Pay bills
- Visit the gym
- Declutter the office

Some of the above tasks will be less appealing to you than others. For example, paying bills is inconvenient, but isn't likely to cause you as much misery as cleaning the bathrooms in your home. Nor does it require as much time and effort as visiting the gym.

So choose a reward that matches the level of dread you feel for the task. For example, paying your bills might only require 10 minutes. Reward yourself by allowing yourself to read your favorite blog for three minutes.

Meanwhile, cleaning the bathrooms in your home might take an hour. Match this task with a larger, more enjoyable reward. For example, allow yourself to read a novel for 30 minutes immediately after completing the chore.

You can also use enjoyable tasks as rewards. For example, you might need to organize a family game night, make a reservation at your favorite restaurant, or plan a birthday party for a friend. Incorporate these tasks into your day along with other rewards.

Here's what the above to-do list might look like:

- Clean the bathrooms

- **Reward:** read novel for 30 minutes
- Visit the grocery store
- **Reward:** organize family game night
- Pay bills
- **Reward:** read favorite blog for three minutes
- Visit the gym
- **Reward:** plan friend's birthday party
- Declutter the office
- **Reward:** watch television for 30 minutes

Enjoy the reward right after you perform the corresponding task. That way, you'll always have something to look forward to.

The above list is just an example, of course. Your list of tasks, rewards, and enjoyable to-do items will vary from my own. It'll not only reflect the things you need to get done on any given day, but also the activities you personally enjoy.

The takeaway is that a smart reward system can spur you to action, and thereby help you to conquer your procrastination habit.

TACTIC #4: FILL YOUR CALENDAR

~

One of the surest ways to guarantee you'll procrastinate is to give yourself too much free time. I speak from experience. If my to-do list has three tasks on it, and I can complete all three within a couple hours, you can bet I'm going to procrastinate. I'll fill up the rest of the time with every manner of distraction.

To be clear, it's fine to plan short, easy days if you have the flexibility. For example, you might plan to work until noon, and spend the rest of the day relaxing. The key is that you *plan* to do so.

The situation I'm referring to above is one for which no such plan exists. You intend to put in a full day of work, but your schedule has large pockets of free time. If you're like me, it's a foregone conclusion that you'll delay taking action on the few tasks you need to complete by the end of the day.

One simple solution is to fill up your calendar. Here's how it works:

Suppose you have eight hours to work with - from 8:00 a.m. to

5:00 p.m. (with an hour for lunch). But you only have three items on your to-do list. You know from experience that you can complete all three tasks in two hours.

That leaves you with six hours of free time. Fill this time with other tasks that need your attention.

You should have at least two to-do lists: one for the current day and a "master list" that contains every task you'll eventually need to address over the coming weeks and months. (Ideally, you should have several lists organized by context. But for the purpose of this section, two lists will suffice.)

Look through your master list. Identify tasks you can work on during your six hours of free time.

One approach is to simply add these tasks to your daily to-do list. But I recommend you also put them on your daily calendar. That way, you can assign time blocks for each one. Your calendar will show you what you should be working on at any given time during your day. That'll encourage you to keep moving forward rather than procrastinate.

I use and recommend Google Calendar for this practice because it's simple, intuitive, and free. But there are many other options.

The most important point to remember is that the less free time you allow yourself, the less likely you'll be to put off tasks. So, if you have a tendency to procrastinate, fill your daily calendar.

TACTIC #5: PRIORITIZE TASKS AND PROJECTS

~

S ome tasks have massive impact. They move the needle in terms of our marriages, careers, income, and other aspects of our lives. Other tasks *seem* important, but actually have little impact on us. They have minimal lasting effect.

When our priorities are vague, or we've prioritized tasks improperly, we end up spending our limited time on the wrong things. The small, inconsequential tasks capture our attention while the larger, more important - and often more difficult - tasks get placed on the back burner.

This happens by way of procrastination. We delay taking action on big items by focusing on smaller, easier ones.

For example, we postpone preparing a big presentation at our job in favor of decluttering our workspace. We delay going to the gym, and instead check our email and return friends' calls. We put off cleaning our houses, choosing instead to shop for gifts for an upcoming birthday party.

In other words, we procrastinate on the big stuff by focusing our attention on the small stuff. We feel like we're getting a lot done, but our important work goes unaddressed.

The solution is to reprioritize the items on your to-do list. Get clear on which tasks are crucial, which are not, and why. Distinguish those that move the needle from those that don't.

There are lots of ways to prioritize tasks. Some people use numbers that range from one to five. "One" signifies a high priority while "five" signifies a low priority. Other folks prefer to use the letters A, B, and C. Still others keep their to-do lists online, and use their respective apps' prioritization feature.

I'm in this latter camp. I use Todoist,[1] which allows me to prioritize tasks with three differently-colored flags (red, orange, and yellow).

The method of prioritization is less important than the practice. Whether you use numbers, letters, or some other device doesn't matter. What matters is that you develop the *habit* of prioritizing each task that appears on your to-do list, and do so in a way that reflects your goals.

This is an important habit regardless of whether you're an executive, entrepreneur, freelancer, stay-at-home parent, or college student. It's how successful people in all walks of life get things done.

On Setting Daily Priorities

Perhaps you already know your priorities in the context of your goals. You know what's important to you. If so, you've already won half the battle. All that's left to do is to assign a priority indicator - one to five, A to C, red flag vs. yellow flag, etc. - to each task on your daily to-do list.

But what if you're not there yet? What if you're uncertain about your priorities? If that's the case, you have more work ahead of you. Don't worry. It's easy, and can even be fun.

Sit down with a pad of paper and pen, and make three columns:

1. Short-term goals
2. Medium-term goals
3. Long-term goals

Next, write down every goal you want to accomplish in the appropriate column. For example, you might write "wash my car" in the short-term column, "write a novel" in the medium-term column, and "retire at 60" in the long-term column.

This sheet of paper, filled with your goals, gives you a roadmap. Use it to gauge the importance of each task that appears on your daily to-do list. Assign a priority level to each item based on whether that item helps you to achieve a specific goal.

How do you prioritize tasks when everything on your to-do list seems critical? First, ask yourself whether this is truly the case. Each task may *seem* critical, but is it? Can some tasks be given a lower priority without resulting in serious consequences? In most cases, you'll find the answer is yes.

Second, distinguish between tasks that are important and tasks that are urgent. Important tasks move you closer to achieving your goals. Urgent tasks just need immediate attention. They may not have any impact on your goals at all.

It's possible to spend all of your time attending to urgent tasks while never attending to the important ones. Focus on those that are both important *and* urgent. Then, focus on the ones that are important, but not urgent. Try to delegate, decline, or postpone all others.

Assigning a priority level to each item on your to-do list clarifies that item's relevance to your goals. Identifying high-priority tasks, and understanding how they impact you, will make you less inclined to put them off.

1. www.Todoist.com

TACTIC # 6: SHORTEN YOUR DAILY TO-DO LIST

∾

Most to-do lists are too long. They contain too many tasks. Consequently, many tasks are left unaddressed and remain unfinished at the end of the day. They must be carried forward to the following day or rescheduled for a future date.

An unfinished to-do list has a demoralizing effect on us. It saps our motivation and injures our egos. And the more unfinished tasks that appear on our lists at the end of the day, the greater their impact.

This problem increases the likelihood that we'll procrastinate. Faced with a long list of tasks and projects at the end of the day, we start to feel overwhelmed, buried under a mountain of unfinished work. Our stress levels rise, and it becomes difficult to make good decisions with regard to how to best allocate our time.

Many people - I'm one of them - respond to this predicament by shutting down. We become paralyzed with inaction. That, of course, exacerbates the problem because it allows unfinished tasks to continue piling up.

The solution is simple: shorten your daily to-do list.

Your daily list should contain no more than seven items. If you include *more* than seven items, there's a high risk that some of them will remain unfinished at the end of the day. At least, that's what I've discovered in my own life.

Seven is doable. It's short enough that your list won't appear unconquerable. Plus, by limiting the number of tasks, you limit the number of conflicting options demanding your attention.

That allows you to focus on the important stuff.

With fewer tasks to focus on, there's less chance you'll procrastinate, whether due to lack of motivation or paralysis stemming from a feeling of overwhelm.

Notes From A Personal Experiment

I've recently been experimenting with to-do lists that contain only three items. I review my "master list" each evening, and pick three tasks to work on the following day. No more than three.

It's important that I pick tasks that fill up my schedule. If I plan to work for eight hours, the three tasks I select should take eight hours to complete. Otherwise, I'll be inclined to loaf around and waste time (see Tactic #4).

So far, this experiment has produced interesting results. I'm able to complete my list each day, which is a great feeling in and of itself. But I've also found that I'm able to complete the three items in less time than they would normally require if they were included on a longer list.

For example, one of my to-do items yesterday was to write 2,000 words. When this task appears on a long to-do list, it takes me approximately five hours to complete (I'm a slow writer). But when it appears as one of only three tasks on my list, I can complete it in three hours.

I realize this effect is a psychological one. Shortening my to-do list doesn't make me more skilled at writing. But I *am* more focused and less stressed. And that makes it easier to roll up my sleeves, ignore distractions, and get into a flow state.

I think you'll find that keeping your to-do list short will have a similar effect on you. Try it and see for yourself.

TACTIC #7: APPLY PARKINSON'S LAW

~

For a lot of people, myself included, the secret to completing a daunting task isn't to throw more time at it. On the contrary, it's to *limit* the time available to work on it. Time constraints cure cognitive inertia. Given a limited amount of time to work on a task, we're more inclined to take focused action toward its completion.

For example, suppose you're a college student and have a chemistry exam next week. Without time constraints, there's little impetus to start studying now. Moreover, when you finally *do* crack open your book and review your class notes, you're almost certain to waste time. The reason is because you haven't placed a time limit on your study session.

In this scenario, you've essentially written yourself a blank check, using time rather than money as currency. Having a unlimited supply - note that it only *seems* unlimited - naturally leads to waste.

Now, consider what happens when your time is limited. Let's

say you give yourself 45 minutes to study for your exam. Two things are likely to happen:

1. **You'll be more focused.** With only 45 minutes to spare, you'll be less prone to distractions.
2. **You'll be more likely to take action.** Allowing yourself 45 minutes to study gives your study session an ending point. This makes the session more fun and less daunting as there's an end in sight.

Parkinson's Law states that *"work expands so as to fill the time available for its completion."* If you give yourself two hours to complete a task, you'll probably take two hours to complete it. Shorten the time available to 90 minutes, and you'll complete the task in that condensed timeframe.

With that principle in mind, set a time limit on every task that appears on your to-do list. That gives each task structure. It also assigns a specific, if artificial, ending point to the task. You'll know in advance how long you'll be working on it.

Next, shorten the time limit you've imposed on yourself. If you initially gave yourself two hours to complete a task, shorten it to 90 minutes. If you initially gave yourself 20 minutes to finish something, shorten it to 15 minutes.

In other words, apply Parkinson's Law.

If you practice these two simple habits, you'll be less inclined to procrastinate, even on tasks and projects you dread. That's because the mind enjoys having an end in sight. When it *has* such an end in sight, it becomes less intimidated by the idea of taking immediate action.

TACTIC #8: ASK OTHERS TO SET YOUR DEADLINES

∿

None of us are strangers to self-imposed deadlines. We regularly set them with every intention of meeting them. But for a variety of reasons, we often fail. This recurrent failure inevitably prompts feelings of guilt. It also raises our stress levels as we fall further and further behind schedule.

First, realize you're not alone. Second, realize there's a solution (more on that in a moment).

Back in 2002, two psychologists, Dan Ariely and Klaus Wertenbroch, conducted a study examining the effect of different types of deadlines on MIT students.[1]

They separated the students into two groups. The first group was asked to submit three papers on a schedule provided for them. The second group was asked to do so based on a schedule they created themselves.

There were a few rules for the second group. First, they had to submit all three papers by the professor's last lecture. Second, they had to share their deadlines with the professor in advance.

Third, they were prohibited from changing the deadlines once they had shared them.

Ariely and Wertenbroch then sat back and watched the experiment unfold.

They expected the second group of students to choose to submit their papers on the day of final lecture. That would give them maximum flexibility; the students could submit their papers early or wait until the last day. It would be up to them.

But that's not what happened. Surprisingly, 75% of the second group set earlier deadlines: one week, four weeks, and six weeks before the semester's end.

This suggested that most of the students in the second group assumed they would procrastinate if given the opportunity. It also suggested they reckoned that setting earlier deadlines would mitigate that inclination.

But again, that's not what happened. The group of students who assigned their own deadlines were more likely to turn their papers in late.

The researchers concluded that performance suffers under self-imposed deadlines. When others set deadlines for us, we tend to perform at a higher level.

Ariely and Wertenbroch conducted a second study that confirmed these findings. In this latter study, subjects with self-imposed deadlines were not only more likely to turn work in late, but they were also less likely to catch errors.

So, if setting your own deadlines doesn't eliminate the risk that you'll procrastinate, who should set them? And how can you encourage these people to help you?

How To Get Others To Set Your Deadlines

The approach you take will depend on your circumstances. If you're a college student, your professor is likely to lay out a schedule detailing when you're expected to turn in assignments and papers, and take exams. But what if your professor expects you to come up with your own schedule?

Ask your professor to do it for you. Tell him or her that you're likely to procrastinate if left to your own devices. Explain that having someone else - presumably, your professor - set your deadlines, and impose consequences for missing them, will spur you to action. That, in turn, will help you get more value from the curriculum.

Use this same approach if you're an executive. If your boss assigns projects to you and expects you to complete them according to a self-imposed schedule, ask him or her to set deadlines for you. Explain to your boss that doing so will make you more accountable, which will improve your timeliness in delivering results.

What if you're an entrepreneur or freelancer? You have neither a professor nor boss to keep you on task. If you're an entrepreneur, seek an accountability partner (we'll talk more about this in *Tactic #10: Be Accountable To Someone*). If you're a freelancer, ask your clients to set (reasonable) due dates for deliverables.

This tactic can work for personal aspects of your life, too. For example, suppose you're in charge of organizing a family vacation. Ask your spouse to set deadlines for you to buy airline tickets, book a hotel room, and plan daily excursions.

Most of us think we can do this on our own. But science says we benefit from others' help in this regard. Try this tactic for yourself. I guarantee it'll help you to tame your inner procrastinator.

---

1. http://journals.sagepub.com/doi/abs/10.1111/1467-9280.00441

TACTIC #9: LEVERAGE YOUR PEAK-ENERGY TIMES OF DAY

∼

I'm an early riser. I wake up at 5:30 a.m. and follow a morning routine that helps me to focus and get started on my work. I've found that I'm more productive and less likely to procrastinate in the early morning. I tend to slow down by 3:00 p.m., and am worthless after 5:00 p.m.

You may be entirely different. You might struggle in the morning, but thrive during the evening. Your creativity and productivity may shoot through the roof as other people like myself are winding down for the day.

The important thing to remember is that our energy levels affect our tendency to procrastinate. So it's worth identifying when your energy levels are at their peak, and making maximum use of those times of day.

How To Identify Your Peak Energy Times

This tactic will require experimentation and patience. But I promise you that the results will make both seem worthwhile.

Follow these three steps to identify your energy levels throughout the day.

Step 1: Create a new spreadsheet. I recommend Google Sheets because it's free and in the cloud so you can access it on your laptop, tablet, or phone.

Step 2: Create the following columns (from left to right):

- Day of the week (Monday, Tuesday, etc.)
- Hourly time block (6:00-7:00 a.m., 7:00-8:00 a.m., etc.)
- Energy rating (1 through 5)
- Notes (detail activities, such as lunch, meetings, etc.)

Step 3: Monitor your energy level. Assign a rating (from one to five) at the end of each time block.

Do Step 3 for a minimum of two weeks. You'll find that patterns will emerge. For example, you might discover that you tend to have a lot of energy between 6:00 a.m. and noon, and little after 5:00 p.m. Or you might discover the opposite: you feel lethargic in the morning and hit your stride after 1:00 p.m.

You may also find that your energy level is heavily influenced by certain activities. For example, meetings might drain your energy while creative work increases it.

The goal of this exercise is to identify the times of day when your energy levels are at their highest point. These are the times when you should schedule difficult or unappealing tasks. You'll be less likely to put them off.

It's worth repeating that this exercise requires patience. Tracking your energy levels on an hourly basis, from morning to evening, for two weeks can be a grind. But there's no better way to gather this data. And once you have it, you'll be able to make better decisions regarding when to schedule tasks you might otherwise be tempted to postpone.

TACTIC #10: BE ACCOUNTABLE TO SOMEONE

∼

We're more likely to get things done when we're accountable to others. It's human nature. We don't want to fail in front of other people. On the contrary, if we tell others we're going to do something, we want to meet that expectation.

For example, suppose you publicly declare that you're going to write and publish a novel in six months' time. You post this declaration on your blog. You announce it on Facebook. You mention it to your coworkers. You tell your family and friends.

All eyes are now on you. You've set an expectation. If you care about how you're perceived, you'll be inclined to start writing your novel. After six months have passed, you don't want to tell everyone that you failed. You want to be able to show them a completed copy of your novel and say "mission accomplished."

That's the power of accountability. We value our social status, and will go to great lengths to improve and reinforce it.

We can use this behavioral impulse to our advantage to help us overcome our tendency to procrastinate. The simple act of telling someone you're going to deliver on a particular task or project serves as an impetus to do so. If we fail to deliver, the person to whom we've made ourselves accountable will call us out on it.

That's a scenario most of us would like to avoid.

For example, suppose you intend to have your car's brake pads replaced. But you're not looking forward to taking your car to the repair shop. Doing so is a major inconvenience. So you're tempted to put it off as long as possible, perhaps to the point that your brakes begin to squeal like banshees.

To counteract the impulse to postpone the repairs, share your intention with someone who will hold you to account. Set a deadline that'll establish whether you've seen the task through.

For example, tell your spouse that you'll take your car into the shop on Saturday morning. If you care about how he or she perceives you in the context of your willingness to follow through on your intentions, you'll do as you had planned.

Being accountable to others spurs us to take action. Again, we want to avoid having to admit failure. Our aversion to doing so gives us the motivation to act.

You can use this tactic on any task or project you're inclined to put off. The key is to find an accountability partner who's willing to hold your feet to the fire. Pick someone you like and trust. It's also helpful if this person is a naturally-positive individual. You want an accountability partner who'll improve your mindset, not weigh you down with negativity.

I strongly encourage you to try this tactic. Don't underestimate its effectiveness. Pick a task you're likely to procrastinate. Commit to completing it by a certain date or time. Share this commitment with a family member, friend, or coworker who'll hold you accountable.

You might be surprised by how motivated you are to take action.

TACTIC #11: TAKE SMALL STEPS

~

S mall tasks are easier to complete than large ones. For example, it's easier to run a sprint than run a marathon. It's easier to write a single scene in a novel than write the entire novel. It's easier to book a hotel room than plan a family vacation from beginning to end.

The larger a task or project is, the more intimidating it seems. This saps our willpower, and makes it difficult to take action.

Think back to when you were in school. Your teacher or professor expected you to write a paper - perhaps a book report, persuasive paper, or expository essay. Whatever the specifics, the project likely seemed daunting at the outset. It involved a lot of time and effort. You needed to perform research; you needed to compile your thoughts into a cohesive form; and ultimately, you needed to turn in a well-written and well thought-out final product.

Thinking about the project in its entirety was probably unsettling, and maybe even disheartening. That being the case, you might have been tempted to put it off. (I did this more times than I can count in high school and college.)

But what happened after you had taken the first step? What happened when you started your research or wrote the first few sentences? I'd be willing to bet the project suddenly became less intimidating. It went from seeming infeasible to seeming doable.

Herein lies an effective tactic for conquering your procrastination habit.

First, break projects down to their smallest parts. Then, treat each part as a separate task. Focus on each one's completion, at which point you can cross it off your to-do list.

For example, let's suppose you're planning to thoroughly clean your home. It's likely to take a few hours and entail a lot of effort, and thus you're tempted to postpone it. Instead of putting it off, let's break the project down, room by room. Here are the individual tasks you'll need to address:

Living room

- Dust furniture
- Vacuum floor
- Wipe down blinds and window treatments
- Declutter coffee table

Dining Room

- Dust/polish dining room table
- Dust chairs
- Vacuum rugs
- Mop floor

Bedrooms

- Vacuum floor
- Empty wastebaskets
- Dust furniture
- Change sheets and bedspread
- Wash windows

Bathrooms

- Clean toilets
- Clean shower/tub
- Wash vanity mirrors
- Declutter vanity surface
- Clean sinks
- Wash floors

Kitchen

- Wash dishes
- Clean countertops
- Mop floor
- Clean appliances
- Clean out refrigerator

Home Office

- Dust furniture
- Organize mail
- Vacuum/sweep floor

- Clean windows

By breaking down this project to its individual components, it becomes less intimidating and more manageable. Yes, there's still a lot to do. That hasn't changed. But you now have a firmer grasp of the smaller tasks that make up the larger project. Moreover, you have a list of individual tasks that can be crossed off when you complete them. That'll give you a continuing sense of accomplishment.

Again, this tactic doesn't lessen the amount of time and effort involved with completing the project. It simply shifts your perspective so the project appears to be more achievable. And that may be all you need to take the first few steps that give you the momentum to finish it.

TACTIC #12: AVOID BORING WORK (WHENEVER POSSIBLE)

~

I n my opinion, boring work is the most difficult work of all. That makes it easy to put off in favor of activities that are more fun or work that's more meaningful.

It's hard to get motivated to do boring work. And once we start working on it, it's difficult to stay focused. Personally, if a boring task takes me more than a few minutes to address, I mentally disengage. I'll complete the task, but my heart won't be in it. Bringing it to completion offers no reward other than the fact that I can finally move on to more engaging tasks and projects.

Perhaps you feel the same way. If so, there's a good chance you procrastinate when faced with such tasks. I certainly do.

The best solution for curbing your procrastination habit in this context is to avoid boring work. Eliminate it from your schedule. If getting rid of it isn't an option, try to delegate it.

For example, suppose you loathe mowing your lawn. You find the task tedious to the point of tears, and if given the option would postpone it indefinitely. In that case, why not delegate the task? Hire someone to mow your lawn for you. That way, it'll get done without your having to motivate yourself to do it.

It may also be possible to replace the boring task with another that's more meaningful to you.

Here's a personal example...

I spent many years writing articles, white papers, case studies, and advertising copy for companies in a variety of industries. Some of the subject matter was fascinating. I'd find myself researching it beyond what was necessary for my clients.

But some of the subject matter was extremely dull to me. I had zero interest in it. Consequently, I faced an enormous amount of internal resistance whenever I sat down to write about it. Often, I'd put off the work until the last minute.

I eventually realized that I didn't have to take on this type of work. I had long since reached the point where I could pick and choose my clients. So, I decided to replace the boring projects with those that held more meaning for me.

The result of this shift in direction was astonishing. I no longer procrastinated on the work I took on. Instead, I was excited to dig in and write the material for my updated stable of clients. I found the work to be more rewarding.

If you're burdened with boring projects, ask yourself whether you can let them go. If you can't get rid of them or delegate them, can you replace them? If doing so is possible, take advantage of that option. You'll find that you're less likely to procrastinate on meaningful work.

What If You Can't Avoid Boring Work?

It won't always be possible for you to avoid boring work, of course. Mundane tasks might be a part of your responsibilities. For example, your boss might expect you to prepare a weekly report that bores you to tears. You can't delegate it, and you can't just let it go. You're forced to grin and bear it.

Or you might be a teacher, and find grading students' essays to be a monotonous (and frustrating) chore. If you lack a classroom aid to foist this task upon, you're stuck having to do it yourself.

If you're stuck with boring work, find a way to make it more engaging.

One solution is to make a game of it. For example, if you're tasked with preparing a dull report for your boss, see how quickly you can finish it without making mistakes. Give yourself a reward if you break your previous time record.

You can also use a "gamification" app to help you work through a to-do list filled with boring tasks. Following are a few examples of such apps:

- Habitica
- LifeRPG
- Task Hammer
- Epic Win
- SuperBetter

These apps are designed to make dull tasks more fun to complete. I don't use them myself, but a lot of users report positive results. You may likewise find these apps make you less inclined to procrastinate.

TACTIC #13: GET RID OF ENVIRONMENTAL DISTRACTIONS

~

Many people assume distractions cause procrastination. But it's the other way around. We *first* choose to procrastinate, and *then* look for things to distract our attention.

This is an important distinction. If we can eliminate items from our environment that serve as distractions, we'll be less likely to put off whatever project we're working on. There wouldn't be anything else in our environment to focus on.

For example, suppose you need to write an article. There are several places in your home in which you can do so.

One option is your living room. The problem is, it has a television, and there's nothing you'd rather do more than watch your favorite shows on Netflix.

Another option is your master bedroom. It doesn't have a TV. But there's a significant amount of clutter. And a cluttered workspace can be just as distracting as a television.

Yet another option is your home office. Like your master bedroom, it doesn't have a TV. Plus, the workspace is clean. For

all intents and purposes, your office is a distraction-free environment. Consequently, if you were to quarantine yourself in your
office, you'd be less likely to procrastinate writing your article.
After all, there would be nothing else for you to focus on.

Here's the important point to remember: the fewer distractions in your environment, the more likely you are to take action
on the task at hand. So it pays to get rid of as many environmental distractions as possible.

Turn off your phone. Clear your workspace. If you're at home,
discourage your family from interrupting you while you work. If
you're at your office, discourage coworkers from dropping by for a
chat. If there are distracting pictures on the walls, remove them. If
there are distracting noises nearby, wear earplugs.

Remember, we first choose to procrastinate. Then, we look for
distractions to fill the freed-up time. Get rid of the distractions in
your environment and minimize the number of outlets through
which to direct your attention. You'll find that it's much more
difficult to justify procrastinating on a project when there's
nothing else to do.

TACTIC #14: GET RID OF DIGITAL DISTRACTIONS

~

Digital distractions can be just as impactful as environmental distractions. In fact, in some cases, they're worse. They're designed to suck you in, and maintain a firm grip on your attention.

Take Facebook as an example.

It's a favored distraction among procrastinators around the globe. Experts estimate the site is responsible for hundreds of billions of dollars in lost productivity each year. That's not by happenstance. Facebook has been designed to hook you, and keep you coming back again and again. It's designed to be addictive.

Nir Eyal, a frequent lecturer at Stanford Graduate School of Business, put it this way:

> *What Facebook wants to create an association with is every time you're bored, every time you have a few minutes. We know that, psychologically speaking, boredom is painful. Whenever you're feeling bored,*

whenever you have a few extra minutes, this is a salve for that itch.[1]

That's a problem if you're a chronic procrastinator. Digital distractions like Facebook constantly tempt you to set aside whatever you're working on in favor of the immediate gratification they offer. This is the reason these types of distractions often trump environmental distractions in terms of impact. They're formulated to be seductive.

For example, our phones have become our constant companions, interrupting us every few minutes with new texts and emails. Social media sites, from Facebook and Twitter to Instagram and Pinterest, tempt us continuously to set our work aside and interact with our friends. The internet offers us an endless list of reasons to procrastinate, from news headlines to YouTube videos.

Unless we take steps to keep them at bay, digital distractions are ever-present, and relentlessly pull at our attention.

Many people convince themselves that they're able to tolerate, and even ignore, these distractions. But evidence suggests that assumption is a delusion - at least for some folks. A study conducted by Timothy Pychyl, author of *Solving The Procrastination Puzzle*, found that 47% of the time people spend online is spent procrastinating.[2]

That's a sobering figure.

Given this finding, I recommend *eliminating* digital distractions rather than simply trying to ignore them.

For example, sever your internet connection whenever you work on your computer. If you need to research something online, don't interrupt your flow to do so. Instead, make a note of it and continue working. Once you've reached an appropriate stopping point, research the needed details and fill in the blanks.

If severing your internet connection isn't an option, use a site-blocking app like SelfControl, Freedom, or StayFocusd. These apps allow you to select an amount of time during which your access to specific websites will be blocked. Addicted to Facebook? Add it to your list of blocked sites. Can't seem to stay away from CNN.com? Block it. Having difficulty staying off Reddit? Put it on the list.

If you need to research something, you can do so without fear that you'll end up squandering an hour on your favorite time-wasting website.

Resist the temptation to check email throughout the day. For example, don't keep a tab open to your email program in your browser. And if you must have your phone on while you work (for example, you're expecting an important call), turn off the notifications that signal the arrival of new emails.

Treat text messages similarly. Ideally, your phone will be off while you work. That way, you won't hear the notifications alerting you of new texts, and won't be tempted to drop what you're doing to read them. If you must keep it on, turn off the notifications.

With the above measures in place, you'll be able to work in peace. You won't be constantly interrupted or seduced by digital distractions. As a result, you'll be less inclined to procrastinate on the task or project at hand.

---

1. http://www.businessinsider.com/science-behind-why-facebook-is-addictive-2014-11
2. http://journals.sagepub.com/doi/abs/10.1177/089443930101900403

TACTIC #15: USE THE TIME CHUNKING METHOD

～

I advocate time chunking. Time chunking is a workflow system that's similar to the Pomodoro Technique. The difference it that it's far more flexible.

Here's how it works:

First, organize tasks according to the type of work they entail and the amount of focus they require. For example, some tasks might involve writing or research. Others, such as paying bills, might entail simple, repetitive actions.

Second, designate a reasonable amount of time to complete each task (or batch of tasks).

Third, create a schedule based on time chunks during which you'll work on the task (or tasks) uninterrupted. Schedule breaks between the time chunks.

For example, suppose you need to write a report. You estimate that you'll need four hours to complete it.

Four hours implies a lot of effort, and consequently you may be tempted to procrastinate. So let's break down the task into manageable time chunks. Here's an example:

- Write for 45 minutes
- Take a 15-minute break
- Write for 45 minutes
- Take a 15-minute break
- Write for 40 minutes
- Take a 10-minute break
- Write for 40 minutes
- Take a 10-minute break
- Write for 35 minutes
- Take a 5-minute break
- Write for 35 minutes
- Celebrate because you've finished writing the paper!

When a large task is broken down into time chunks, it becomes less intimidating. Moreover, the promise of regular breaks between each time chunk makes the task seem less unpleasant and more doable.

Personally, I would dread having to sit down for four hours to write a report. But write for 45 minutes followed by a 15-minute break? Write for 40 minutes followed by a 10-minute break? That's no problem at all.

And thus the work would get done.

Don't rely on a wall clock. When working in time chunks, I recommend that you use a timer. A $5 kitchen timer is fine. You might prefer to use your phone, but be wary of the distractions your phone might introduce - for example, email, text, and social media notifications.

Place the timer in front of you. Set it according to the amount of time you've allotted for your next time chunk (e.g. 45 minutes). Then, work on the task or project at hand until the timer goes off, signaling the time chunk has ended. Don't stop working until this happens.

Once the timer goes off, set it for the amount of time you've allotted for your next break (e.g. 15 minutes). Spend that time doing anything you desire, including any of the time-wasting activities you might have pursued in lieu of working on the task at hand. Read your favorite blogs. Check Facebook. Watch a few YouTube videos. Take a power nap.

When the timer goes off, set it for the duration of your next time chunk and get back to work.

Working in this manner will lessen the temptation to procrastinate. It breaks down big, daunting projects into more manageable pieces. Moreover, working for short periods of time improves your focus, making you less susceptible to distractions.

Try time chunking the next time you're faced with a task or project that's likely to require more than two hours to complete. You may be surprised by how willing you are to get started when a break is right around the corner.

TACTIC #16: ELIMINATE AS MANY UNNECESSARY TASKS AS POSSIBLE

～

As noted earlier, we're more likely to procrastinate when we have a lot of options. We touched on this tendency in *Part I: Why We Procrastinate* (*Options That Promise More Immediate Gratification*). But in that section, we limited the discussion to distractions, such as social media, YouTube, and television.

Other tasks can have the same effect. If we're forced to choose between working on a difficult task and an easy one, most of us would be tempted to choose the latter.

You know this from firsthand experience. You've no doubt reviewed your to-do list at times, and gravitated toward items that promised to take comparatively less time and effort. I've done this more times than I can count.

In this way, easy tasks tempt us to procrastinate on difficult ones.

Such tasks are sometimes unavoidable. You may not need to address them right away, but you'll need to address them at some point during your day. For example, you might need to call a customer, email your child's teacher, or pay this month's bills. These tasks need attention, but rarely do they need *immediate* attention. They can be scheduled on your daily calendar and addressed based on priority.

Other tasks are entirely unnecessary. They don't move the needle in terms of helping you to achieve your goals. As such, they're a waste of time and effort.

You can probably relate to this problem, as well. Have you ever created a to-do list that was so long that you knew you'd never be able to finish every item? Have you ever looked at your to-do list and wondered why some of the items were even listed?

I used to regularly encounter these problems. Years ago, my to-do lists weren't properly organized by context. They were just a massive inventory of tasks that I'd write down as they came to mind. A large number were unimportant. They could disappear from my lists, and I'd never notice.

These nonessential tasks were appealing to my inner procrastinator because they were often simple to perform, and required little time and effort to complete. I would frequently put off more difficult, more important tasks in favor of working on these insignificant ones. It was a form of stalling.

I eventually overhauled my to-do list system. One of my top priorities was to never allow trivial tasks to appear on my daily lists. I also reviewed my lists throughout each day, looking for items that were made irrelevant and could be eliminated without impact.

An interesting thing happened. First, my daily to-do list shrank in size, from dozens of items to fewer than seven. Second, and most importantly, this dramatic reduction gave me fewer options through which to justify procrastinating on difficult tasks.

My to-do lists are even smaller today. As I mentioned in *Tactic #6: Shorten Your Daily To-Do List*, I'm experimenting with lists that contain only three items. The effect on my inner procrastinator has been even more pronounced. Faced with only a few tasks, I'm unable to justify wasting time on nonessential items.

I recommend you review your to-do list each morning. Look for trivial tasks that have a negligible effect on whether you achieve your goals. Eliminate them. In doing so, you'll rid your list of items that serve only to tempt you to put off more significant, consequential tasks.

TACTIC #17: FOCUS ON ONE TASK AT A TIME

~

Most of us multitask. We juggle more than one item at a time, believing that doing so helps us to get more done. But most of us know intuitively that such an outcome is unrealistic. Multitasking erodes our focus, makes us more prone to distractions, increases our error rate, and lessens our productivity.

But there's another reason to abandon the practice: it makes us more likely to procrastinate. Juggling multiple tasks and projects makes us *feel* as if we're getting a lot done. We relish that feeling of accomplishment. The problem is, it's usually an illusion. We keep ourselves busy with trivial tasks, but overlook - or worse, actively ignore - more important tasks.

In other words, multitasking is often a form of procrastination.

Social writer Clay Shirky put it best when he said the following in an article he wrote for Medium.com:

 People often start multi-tasking because they believe it

will help them get more done. Those gains never materialize; instead, efficiency is degraded. However, it provides emotional gratification as a side-effect. (Multitasking moves the pleasure of procrastination inside the period of work.) [1]

That last sentence is worth repeating. *"Multitasking moves the pleasure of procrastination inside the period of work."*

This is a seductive effect that greatly influences our behavior. The illusion of productivity fills us with positive feelings. We feel emotionally satisfied when we *think* we're getting a lot done. These feelings encourage us to repeat whatever action we took that prompted them.

So we keep multitasking. This is the reason it's so difficult to curb the habit. But curb it you must if you truly want to stop procrastinating. For the two habits - delaying action and multitasking - are inextricably linked.

How To Become A Single-Tasker

Single-tasking is a habit like any other. So be patient with yourself as you develop it. Take small steps and build on them over time.

First, if you're not already doing so, I strongly recommend working from a daily to-do list. Don't rely on your memory. Write down every item that needs your attention. The fewer the better because, as we noted earlier, that reduces your options and increases your focus.

Second, give each task on your to-do list a priority level. Use numbers (one, two, or three), letters (A, B, or C), or the prioritization feature of the task management app of your choice.

Third, prioritize tasks the night before. That way, you won't waste time doing so on the day you need to complete them. You can simply look at your list, identify the high-priority items, and focus your attention on them before addressing less-important work.

Fourth, clear your workspace of distractions, both environmental and digital. We covered this topic in detail in *Tactics #13 and #14.*

Fifth, schedule your day in time chunks (discussed in *Tactic #15*). Working in time chunks will encourage you to focus on one task at a time.

Sixth, if you're constantly tempted to multitask online, close all but one browser tab. You'll be less susceptible to the unending stream of distractions available on the internet.

Seventh, each time you switch from one task to another - that's what multitasking is - recognize the cost associated with the interruption. This is known as a switching cost. It can have a devastating effect on your productivity.

Remember, single-tasking is a habit. The best way to make it stick is to develop it slowly. This is especially true if, like most folks, you've been a lifelong multitasker. So take your time, be patient with yourself, and forgive the occasional stumbles. The upside is that you'll enjoy more focus, greater productivity, and be less inclined to procrastinate.

---

1. https://medium.com/@cshirky/why-i-just-asked-my-students-to-put-their-laptops-away-7f5f7c50f368

TACTIC #18: PURGE NEGATIVE SELF-TALK

～

S elf-talk is internal dialogue about yourself. It heavily influences how you perceive yourself, to the point that you may believe things that are untrue.

For example, you might repeatedly tell yourself that you're a failure, and consequently believe that anything you try to do is bound to fail. Defining yourself as a failure is certain to be an unfair and inaccurate portrayal. Yet this pervasive, unchallenged self-perception can ultimately convince you that any project you undertake will end in disappointment.

That increases the temptation to procrastinate. After all, no one relishes the prospect of failure. We're inclined to avoid it, even if that means indefinitely putting off projects we believe will ultimately lead to our defeat.

Negative self-talk comes in a variety of forms. The most obvious form is self-criticism. We berate ourselves about perceived flaws, comparing ourselves unfavorably to people we consider to be superior to us in those areas. This practice pummels our self-esteem to the point that it becomes difficult to take action on anything.

Constant worrying is another form of negative self-talk. We spend an inordinate amount of time and energy agonizing over self-fabricated falsehoods, or about things over which we have little control. We anticipate the worst possible scenario. Is it any wonder that the constant worrier procrastinates?

Yet another form of negative self-talk is perfectionism. We consider anything that's less than perfect to be unacceptable. Meanwhile, we know intuitively that, being human, we're intrinsically imperfect. Holding ourselves to an impossible standard discourages us from taking action.

Because negative self-talk can have such a significant impact on our behavior, it's important to squash it whenever it surfaces.

First, identify the areas of your life where you habitually engage in negative self-talk. For example, you might do it whenever you think about the relationships you share with your friends. Or you might entertain negative thoughts about yourself with respect to getting into shape. Or you may constantly burden yourself with negative self-talk in the context of your job performance.

Second, learn to identify negative self-talk in all its various forms. For example, if something bad happens, and you instinctively blame yourself, recognize that as negative self-talk. If you're about to start a task, and immediately expect the worst to happen, recognize *that* as negative self-talk.

Third, whenever you have negative thoughts about yourself, put a positive, realistic spin on them. For example, suppose you're procrastinating on a project because you're convinced you'll do a less-than-perfect job on it. Remind yourself that no one is perfect, and no reasonable person expects perfection. Moreover, an imperfect job may exceed everyone's expectations.

Make this practice a habit so it becomes an automatic response to the negative self-dialogue.

Fourth, surround yourself with supportive people. For example, if you're hobbled by perfectionism, it's good to have a friend who'll tell you, *"Nobody expects you to be perfect. Focus, trust your ability, and I'm sure you'll do a fantastic job."*

Eliminating negative self-talk won't happen overnight. It'll take time. But if you consistently challenge every negative internal thought about yourself, you'll find that doing so becomes easier and easier. Along the way, you'll become more positive, more optimistic about your abilities, and increasingly willing to take action.

TACTIC #19: LIMIT YOUR OPTIONS TO ONE

$\sim$

This tactic is related to *Tactic #16: Eliminate As Many Unnecessary Tasks As Possible*. But here, we're not merely focused on purging your daily to-do list of trivial items. We're interested in taking a more drastic approach.

First, it's important to acknowledge the role of choice in our lives. Most of us have the freedom to spend our time in a multitude of ways. Whether we're relaxing at home or working at the office, there's no shortage of options vying for our attention. Some of those options offer immediate gratification, tempting us to put off important work that offers less gratification in the present.

For example, suppose you're working online. One of your high-priority tasks is to read a scientific paper for something related to your job. The paper is long and information-dense, and thus promises to require a lot of time and effort.

If you're like me, you have multiple tabs open in your browser. Each one is an option that distracts you from the task at hand. In this scenario, the temptation to procrastinate reading the scientific paper in favor of reading content that delivers more immediate gratification is irresistible.

The solution is to eliminate all options unrelated to the task at hand. In this example, that means closing all browser tabs except the one that's open to the scientific paper.

Here's another example:

Suppose you're in your office preparing an important presentation. The problem is, it's difficult work, and thus you're susceptible to distractions. You have other options regarding how to spend your time, including checking your email, listening to your voicemail, attending an upcoming meeting, or visiting a coworker's office to chat.

These options are an excuse to postpone preparing your presentation. None of them have as high a priority.

One solution to this problem is to grab a pen and paper, and quarantine yourself in a conference room. Leave your computer and phone behind. Doing so eliminates your options, forcing you to focus your attention on your presentation. It's difficult to procrastinate on the task in front of you when you have nothing else to do.

Whenever possible, reduce your options to one - ideally, the most important task on your to-do list. Then, use time chunking to designate periods during which you can focus 100% of your attention on that task.

I'll end this section with an interesting story I learned about the acclaimed French novelist Victor Hugo. He struggled with procrastination. Hugo did much of his writing in Paris, a city filled with bars, cafes, parks, and walking trails. These options constantly tempted him to set aside his work.

Hugo realized that going outside would negatively impact his writing productivity. So he came up with a solution. Confining himself to his study, he undressed each day and asked his servant to hide his clothes. He further instructed his servant to return his clothes at a specific time, at which point Hugo estimated he would have completed his work for the day.

By surrendering his clothes, Hugo eliminated his options. He forced himself to remain in his study for the amount of time he needed to complete that day's writing session.

I think he was on to something.

The next time you find yourself procrastinating, eliminate every option unrelated to the task you're putting off. Left with a single option, you'll find it's much easier to start working on it.

TACTIC #20: FIGURE OUT WHY YOU'RE PROCRASTINATING

∽

In *Part I: Why We Procrastinate*, we covered more than a dozen reasons we put things off. Not all of them will describe your personal circumstances. But at least a few undoubtedly will.

It's not enough to understand the reasons people procrastinate. It's imperative that you also identify your *personal* triggers. Only then can you take purposeful action to overcome them.

For example, are you fearful of failure? Or are you fearful of success? Each warrants a different set of remedies.

Or perhaps you tend to procrastinate when you feel either overwhelmed or bored (both common triggers). Each of these obstacles entails a different resolution - a different course of treatment, as it were.

Maybe you have a low tolerance for adversity, which paralyzes you when things don't go your way, but have never had a problem making decisions. Or perhaps it's the other way around. You can tolerate a great deal of adversity, but making decisions has always been difficult for you. The road to recovery will look different in each scenario.

Throughout *Part I: Why We Procrastinate*, I highlighted my personal albatrosses. I noted that perfectionism was a major obstacle for me in the past. I also mentioned that I've always had an aversion to trying new things. Further, I pointed out that I used to have a low tolerance for adverse events.

It was necessary for me to identify these triggers as personal obstacles before I could take steps to resolve them. Likewise, I strongly encourage *you* to consider the reasons *you* procrastinate.

How To Identify Your Personal Triggers

It's difficult to call to mind the cues that prompt you to behave in a particular way. For this reason, I recommend monitoring your triggers as they occur. Track them for two weeks at a minimum.

Here's how:

Whenever you feel you're about to procrastinate, stop and evaluate your mental state. Ask yourself what's preventing you from taking action in that moment. If you need a place to start, review the list in *Part I: Why We Procrastinate*.

Once you've identified the trigger, write it down. Note there may be more than one. If so, write down all of them.

Over the course of two weeks, you'll see patterns emerge. For example, you might notice that you tend to procrastinate due to laziness. Or you may discover you regularly put things off because you hold yourself to unrealistically high standards (perfectionism).

The purpose of this exercise is to pinpoint your personal triggers. Once you've done so, you can take steps toward making impactful changes.

TACTIC #21: PERFORM A WEEKLY AUDIT OF YOUR GOALS

~

I enthusiastically advocate performing personal weekly audits. They help to ensure you spend your time and effort in the most productive manner possible given your short, medium, and long-term goals.

I also advocate using multiple to-do lists to manage tasks and projects. At a minimum, you should maintain a *daily* to-do list and a *master* to-do list. Ideally, your master list would feed one or more contextual lists so you can better manage your workload.

One of the most common problems people face in maintaining their master and contextual to-do lists is that their lists grow too long. New tasks and projects are added each day, eventually making these lists unworkable.

Some of these tasks and projects are important and addressed accordingly. Others are unimportant, yet manage to stick around for weeks, and even months, on end. With time, they become a burden. They're unnecessary and do nothing more than create clutter. The more cluttered your to-do list, the more likely you are to feel overwhelmed by the mountain of work it imposes upon you.

This feeling of overwhelm is a common trigger for procrastination, as we discussed at length in *Part I: Why We Procrastinate.*

A weekly audit gives you a simple way to actively manage this problem. It helps you to focus your time and effort on important work rather than feeling buried under a wave of tasks that range from significant to trivial.

While performing your weekly audit, you'll identify which tasks are essential to your goals, and which can be eliminated without impact. You'll also have an opportunity to reprioritize tasks as your goals rise and fall in importance.

The purpose of this exercise is to declutter your to-do lists. By reviewing your goals each week, you can quickly assess which tasks and projects can be jettisoned without consequence. That will keep your lists clean, organized, and less likely to overwhelm you.

As you go through your week with clean lists, you'll feel less burdened by your workload. You'll be able to focus on fewer items, knowing their completion will help you to reach your goals rather than needlessly consume your limited time.

And that may be one of the keys to helping you to finally conquer your procrastination habit.

BONUS TACTIC #1: USE TEMPTATION BUNDLING

$\sim$

Temptation bundling probably sounds strange if you've never heard of it. The phrase was coined by Katherine Milkman, PhD, professor at the Wharton School of Business.

It came about when Milkman was trying, and failing, to stick to an exercise routine. At the time, she had a passion for fiction novels like *The Hunger Games*. So she bundled the temptation to read such novels with the practice of going to the gym. To that end, she would only allow herself to read her novels of choice if she first completed her daily workout.

It worked. She found that bundling one of her favorite activities (reading fiction) with a habit she had difficulty making stick (exercising) was successful. She began to visit the gym five days a week, spurred by the promise that she would get to read her favorite books.

Milkman describes temptation bundling as *"coupling instantly-gratifying 'want' activities with engagement in a 'should behavior' that provides long-term benefits but requires the exertion of willpower."*

In other words, reward yourself for doing something you should be doing.

Temptation bundling has practical value outside mere habit development. You can also use it to curb your inner procrastinator.

For example, suppose you've been putting off cleaning out your garage. It's a big task that's bound to take a significant amount of time. Moreover, your garage is hot and dusty. To say you're not looking forward to the chore is an understatement.

Meanwhile, let's also suppose you love binge-watching *The Sopranos, Game of Thrones, Downton Abbey,* and *Law & Order: SVU.* You love doing so to the point that you're tempted to do it in lieu of cleaning out your garage.

Bundle the chore (cleaning your garage) with your desired activity (binge-watching your favorite TV show). Use the latter as a reward for completing the former. In other words, motivate yourself to do what you *should* do with the promise of something you *want* to do. Assuming you're sufficiently motivated by the reward, you'll be inclined to take action on the task at hand rather than put it off.

Watch Milkman talking about temptation bundling in this video.[1] It's short at just over five minutes.

How To Create A Temptation Bundling System

You need two lists. The first will include tasks you need to get done. The second will include activities you want to do (i.e. your rewards).

You probably already have the first list in front of you. This is your daily to-do list. The next step is to compile the second list (the rewards list). Here are some of the activities that might appear on it:

- Watch your favorite television program
- Play your favorite video game
- Spend time on Facebook
- Visit Starbucks and enjoy your favorite drink
- Go for a walk
- Visit a nearby shopping mall and buy a new shirt or blouse
- Meet a friend for lunch

Once you have both lists in front of you, all that remains is to match each task you're tempted to postpone with a rewarding activity. The reward should offer a level of instant gratification that's proportionate to the time and effort required to complete the to-do item.

For example, meeting a friend for lunch might be a reasonable reward for cleaning out your garage. But it's too large a reward for emptying your kitchen trash.

I've found temptation bundling to be highly effective in curbing my tendency to procrastinate. I recommend you experiment with it. You may find it's a great tool for prompting yourself to take action on tasks you're otherwise inclined to put off.

---

1. https://www.youtube.com/watch?v=snHnUc9Yudk

BONUS TACTIC #2: USE COMMITMENT DEVICES

~

W e touched on the use of commitment devices in previous tactics, but didn't define them as such. Let's do that now.

A commitment device is anything that restricts your behavior or limits the manner in which you spend your time.

For example, suppose you and your friend plan to visit your favorite restaurant. Further suppose you're on a diet, and want to resist the temptation to indulge in dessert. You might give your friend $100 with the understanding that he or she can keep it if you eat dessert.

That's a type of a commitment device.

Another example: suppose you do most of your work online. The problem is, you're constantly distracted by social media, email, and YouTube, each of which is one click away. To keep such distractions at bay, you decide to use a website blocker, such as Self-Control, StayFocusd, or FocusBooster.

The website blocker is a type of commitment device.

The term was coined by Steven Levitt and Stephen J. Dubner,

authors of the bestselling non-fiction book *Freakonomics*. They defined a commitment device as follows:

 A means with which to lock yourself into a course of action that you might not otherwise choose but that produces a desired result.

Commitment devices limit your options. They allow your rational self, the one who knows what you should be doing and possesses the good sense to act accordingly, to take the reins. They relegate your *irrational* self, the one who's inclined to put off important tasks in favor of those that promise immediate gratification, to the backseat.

The constraints that commitment devices impose on our behavior can prove invaluable in spurring us to take purposeful action. Rather than being forced to choose how to allocate our time among competing options, we're left with few of them. Ideally, we're left with only one: the task at hand.

For example, suppose you need to prepare a presentation for your job. You estimate the task will take two hours to complete. The challenge is, you'd rather spend the time watching YouTube videos, reading the news, or chatting with coworkers. Here's one way to use a commitment device to help ensure you stay on task.

Step 1: visit StickK.com and select a goal (e.g. complete your presentation within two hours).

Step 2: Set the stakes (e.g. $100).

Step 3: Designate a referee. Choose a coworker, your boss, or administrative assistant - someone who can keep an eye on you.

Step 4: Inform the person you've chosen as the referee of his or her role.

If you complete your presentation within two hours, you won't be out any money.

If you fail to meet your goal, however, your referee will be notified by StickK.com and asked to verify the outcome. Your credit card will then be charged $100 (the stakes you chose).

With this particular commitment device, you can put off your presentation and spend the time watching videos, reading current events, and chatting with coworkers. But doing so comes at a price - notably, a price set by you. If the stakes are high enough, you'll feel compelled to work on your presentation.

Commitment devices aren't a recent invention as an inducement to take action. You may remember reading about the Spanish conquistador Hernán Cortés in school. In 1521, before marching on Tenochtitlan, the capital of the Aztec Empire, Cortés burned and sunk his ships. Doing so limited the options available to his men, whom he feared might otherwise mutiny. With their ships sunk, they had no choice but to move forward.

Thankfully, the stakes for most of us are less serious today. Even so, commitment devices can be highly useful in helping us to conquer our inner procrastinators. If you're tempted to postpone an important project in favor of enjoying immediate gratification, set up a commitment device. It'll keep you on task, encouraging you to work on the project you're trying to put off.

BONUS TACTIC #3: FORGIVE YOURSELF

~

I f you've read any of my other books, you know that I'm a huge advocate of self-forgiveness. In my opinion, it's incredibly important to show yourself kindness whenever you mishandle a situation. Berating yourself is unlikely to help matters.

This is definitely the case when you procrastinate. In fact, scolding yourself is likely to make things worse. After all, making yourself feel like a failure is hardly good motivation for effecting positive changes.

It bears repeating that procrastination is a habit. It's learned over time and reinforced each time we do it. After years of practice, it becomes deeply rooted in our brains. It becomes part of our daily process. We instinctively look for ways to postpone taking action on unappealing tasks.

Breaking this entrenched habit won't happen overnight. It took years to develop, and will take time to curb.

Along the way, you're almost certain to experience minor

setbacks. That's okay! Forgive yourself, recommit, and take another step forward.

Study Suggests Self-Forgiveness Is Crucial To Curbing Procrastination

The notion that self-forgiveness can help break the procrastination habit has scientific support. In 2010, a study was conducted by Michael Wohl, a psychology professor at Carlton University in Canada, Timothy Pychyl, the aforementioned author of *The Procrastination Puzzle*, and psychiatrist Shannon Bennet. They asked the question *"If we self-forgive after we procrastinate, do we procrastinate less the next time we face a similar task?"*

To answer this question, Wohl and his colleagues followed 134 first-year college students tasked with preparing for two successive exams. The students were asked to report on four items:

1. whether they procrastinated studying for the first exam.
2. their feelings of guilt for having done so.
3. whether they forgave themselves.
4. whether they procrastinated studying for the second exam.

Wohl, Pychyl, and Bennet noted the effects of self-forgiveness following the students' decision to procrastinate studying for the first exam. They focused on whether this self-forgiveness lessened the students' feelings of guilt and emotional distress, and how it affected their tendency to procrastinate studying for the *second* exam.

Wohl and his colleagues found that the students who were willing to forgive themselves were more likely to change their future behavior. To wit, they were less likely to put off studying for the second exam.

The researchers came to the following conclusion:

> *Forgiveness allows the individual to move past maladaptive behavior and focus on the upcoming examination without the burden of past acts to hinder studying... By realizing that procrastination was a transgression against the self and letting go of negative affect associated with the transgression via self-forgiveness, the student is able to constructively approach studying for the next exam.*[1]

That's a fancy way of saying that self-forgiveness for a first act of procrastination reduces the likelihood that a second act will occur.

The Takeaway: Forgive Yourself

Science and research aside, you probably know from experience that rebuking yourself for putting off a project doesn't result in long-term behavioral change. If anything, it just makes you feel badly about your decisions.

Forgiving yourself gives you an opportunity to accept responsibility for your decisions, face the accompanying twinge of regret, and most importantly to move forward, committed to acting differently down the road.

This process can help tame the beast of procrastination where self-blame will only make it more ferocious.

Coming Up Next...

We've just covered two dozen tactics you can use to overcome the procrastination habit. But is it possible that there are times when procrastination is actually *helpful*? The answer, found in the following pages, may surprise you.

1. http://www.sciencedirect.com/science/article/pii/S0191886910000474

PART III

WHEN PROCRASTINATION HELPS YOU TO GET THINGS DONE

~

Thus far, we've talked about procrastination as an obstacle to getting things done. But there's more to the story. Sometimes, procrastination is helpful, and it makes sense to *embrace* it rather than try to curb it.

That may sound counterintuitive. We usually think of putting things off in the context of how it negatively affects our productivity. But in the following few pages, I'll introduce you to a form of procrastination that can actually help you to be *more* productive.

The material that follows isn't meant to give you license to put things off arbitrarily. Its purpose isn't to enable your inner procrastinator. On the contrary, introducing you to this variant of "traditional" procrastination will help you to better structure your day according to the tasks you plan to address.

If the above sounds confusing, don't worry. Everything will become clearer in the next few moments.

Let's jump in...

THE ART OF ACTIVE PROCRASTINATION

∼

The term "active procrastination" sounds like an oxymoron, like "tragic comedy" or "open secret." The act of postponing tasks and projects implies inaction. So how can the practice be *active*?

The answer is best captured by a quote from the American humorist Robert Benchley...

> *Anyone can do any amount of work, provided it isn't the work he's supposed to be doing at that moment.*

If the most important thing you have to do today is sufficiently daunting, you'll look for other things to do in its stead. The *passive* procrastinator will fill the time with activities that promise immediate gratification. He or she gives little consideration to task prioritization.

The *active* procrastinator will address other tasks he or she deems to be just as important as - and more urgent than - the original task.

For example, suppose you plan to give your home a thorough cleaning. You estimate the "project" will take three hours and require a lot of effort. To say you're dreading it is an understatement.

If you're a *passive* procrastinator, you might postpone the housecleaning in favor of binge-watching your favorite shows on Netflix.

If you're an *active* procrastinator, you'll postpone the housecleaning, and use the time to pay bills, visit the grocery store, and prepare dinner. You're choosing to address tasks that are just as important as cleaning your home, but arguably more urgent.

As an active procrastinator, you'll eventually get around to the housecleaning, especially if you've given yourself a deadline. You might finish it with mere moments to spare, but the "project" will get done.

That's active procrastination in a nutshell. Researchers have found the practice can have a positive effect on how we use our time.[1]

How Active Procrastination Increases Your Productivity

Active procrastination is particularly well-suited for folks who thrive under pressure. Further, these individuals are adept at deciding how to allocate their time among competing options based on the respective priorities of those options.

This is far different than the traditional procrastinator who wastes time doing things he or she shouldn't be doing. Active procrastinators don't visit YouTube to watch videos when they put off intimidating or unpleasant tasks. They address *other* important tasks.

In this way, the disciplined active procrastinator is highly productive. Everything on his or her to-do list gets finished, although perhaps not in the order originally planned.

Moreover, because active procrastinators put themselves in a position where they must work under pressure, they're less likely to be hobbled by perfectionism. They implicitly give themselves permission to do an imperfect job.

It's worth noting that not all productivity experts buy into the notion that active procrastination leads to positive outcomes. For example, the aforementioned Timothy Pychyl, author of *The Procrastination Puzzle*, has opined that procrastination, at its heart, is a failure of self-regulation. To that end, he notes the following...

> *Other examples of self-regulatory failure include problem drinking, compulsive gambling, or shopping, and over-eating. Can you imagine putting the adverb "active" in front of these words to describe some positive aspect of this behavior? I don't think so.* [2]

Although I enjoy Pychyl's work on the subject of procrastination, I disagree with the above premise. I believe self-regulatory failure in the context of active procrastination isn't as disastrous as he implies. As active procrastinators, we're capable of putting off tasks and still completing a tremendous amount of work. To that end, active procrastination, when applied properly, can potentially boost our productivity.

I know this from experience. I'm willing to bet that you do, as well.

---

1. https://www.ncbi.nlm.nih.gov/pubmed/15959999
2. https://www.psychologytoday.com/blog/dont-delay/200907/active-procrastination-thoughts-oxymorons

BONUS MATERIAL: ANSWERS TO COMMON QUESTIONS ABOUT OVERCOMING PROCRASTINATION

∽

You may have started reading *The Procrastination Cure* with a number of questions concerning how to conquer your inner procrastinator. It's my hope that the material we've covered thus far has answered most, if not all, of those questions.

Having said that, you may have a few residual concerns that warrant more attention. I'll try to address them below by answering the most common questions I've been asked by subscribers to my productivity newsletter.

"I'm a lifelong procrastinator. Can I really overcome this bad habit?"

Absolutely! I'm a reasonably good case study.

By college, I had practically turned the practice of procrastination into an art form. I postponed anything that held even the slightest hint of hard work or unpleasantness. It was a "skill" I had honed since childhood.

I eventually turned the corner thanks largely to the tactics I shared with you in *Part II: 21 Ways To Beat Your Inner Procrastinator.*

It didn't happen overnight. In fact, it took me several months to define my priorities, evaluate my failings, and finally learn how to consistently take action.

If I could do it, you *definitely* can do the same. In fact, I wouldn't be surprised if it took you far less time.

The important thing to remember is that taking action, the nemesis of procrastination, is a habit. Like any habit, developing it takes time.

I'm a big believer in taking small steps when incorporating a new habit or routine in your life. That's the best way to acclimate your mind (and sometimes your body) and make the habit stick.

I recommend that you spend one week incorporating each of the tactics I shared with you in *Part II*. Make each one a separate habit. By the time you reach the end of *Part II*, you'll have mastered the tools you need to finally control your inner procrastinator.

"I'm constantly distracted by social media, and end up procrastinating important work. How can I beat my social media addiction?"

In my opinion, the best way to overcome a social media addiction is to use a three-pronged approach...

Prong #1: Turn off your phone notifications.

Prong #2: Impose time restrictions on yourself.

Prong #3: Spend more time with people in "real life."

Having said that, the important thing is to identify *why* social media is causing you to procrastinate your work. You can visit Facebook at any time. Why do you choose to do it when an important task or project looms?

I'd venture to say the reason (or reasons) can be found in *Part I: Why We Procrastinate.*

For example, you might be paralyzed by a fear of failure. Instead of tackling the task at hand, you choose to check out what's happening on Twitter.

Or you may feel saddled with negative self-talk. Instead of challenging the negative thoughts and pressing forward, you choose to visit Instagram or Pinterest.

The point is, curbing your social media addiction in this scenario may not resolve your tendency to procrastinate. If your inner procrastinator is driven by some other trigger, you'll find some other way to distract yourself.

I recommend that you revisit *Part I: Why We Procrastinate.* Ask yourself whether any of the items listed in that section play an influential role in your life. If so, focus on resolving those items. You may find that your social media addiction isn't nearly the distraction you imagined.

"I've successfully completed a project I've been dreading. How do I keep the momentum going?"

Congratulations! Take a moment to celebrate that victory. It may seem like a small thing in the moment, but acknowledging your accomplishment will make you feel great. And that'll encourage you to take action again and again until doing so becomes a deeply-rooted habit.

Each time you cross a task off your to-do list, you'll enjoy a rewarding sense of achievement. Use it as fuel to keep going!

"I procrastinate because I feel overwhelmed. How do I fix this problem?"

As we noted in *Part I: Why We Procrastinate,* a feeling of overwhelm is a common trigger for procrastination. Confronted by a tidal wave of tasks, we become paralyzed with inaction.

I've found the best way to overcome this cognitive paralysis is to make a list and start tackling the easiest tasks first.

For example, suppose you have dozens of things to do and you're feeling swamped. Here's how I'd handle it...

Step #1: Put every to-do item on a list.

Step #2: Identify the items that must be done today. Put these on a separate list, crossing them off the first list.

Step #3: Rank today's to-do items according to the ease with which they can be completed.

Step #4: Start with the easiest item. Then, do the next-easiest time. And so forth.

I normally advocate "eating the frog," or doing the most dreadful task first (see *Tactic #1* in *Part II: 21 Ways To Beat Your Inner Procrastinator*). But if you're feeling overwhelmed, it's more important to get started and build some momentum. The best way to do that is to focus only on tasks that need to be done today, and tackle the lowest-hanging fruit.

Completing the easy tasks first will whittle down your to-do list while filling you with a sense of achievement. That'll make you feel less overwhelmed. It'll also inspire you to tackle the more difficult or time-consuming tasks on your list.

"I'm a chronic procrastinator. Instead of fighting the urge to procrastinate, can't I just practice active procrastination?"

Maybe. But probably not.

If you remember our discussion about active procrastination, you'll recall there's a crucial difference between passive and active procrastinators. The former put off tasks without any sense of prioritization. They do it in pursuit of short-term gratification.

Active procrastinators put off tasks to work on other important tasks. It's not merely a failure of self-regulation; it's a delaying tactic, which, thanks in part to the adrenaline rush that comes with working under pressure, leads to increased productivity.

Most chronic procrastinators are *passive* procrastinators. I certainly was. It would not have been an easy transition for me from passive to active. In fact, had I chosen to abandon my goal of overcoming my inner procrastinator, and instead immediately adopt the practice of active procrastination, it would have been a disaster.

If you're interested in practicing active procrastination, I recommend you first curb your tendency to put things off. Only after you've gained control over that aspect of your life, experiment with active procrastination.

YOU MAY HAVE other questions regarding how to conquer your inner procrastinator. It's difficult for me to foretell the nature of those questions. I encourage you to reach out me at damon@artofproductivity.com.

FINAL THOUGHTS ON CONQUERING PROCRASTINATION

~

If you're struggling to manage your procrastination habit, you're not alone. All of us have faced the same struggle. In fact, we continue to face it every single day. Curbing the habit is like the experience described by recovering alcoholics seeking long-term sobriety: there's an ever-present temptation to "slip." The potential for relapse is a constant.

Don't be discouraged by this fact. The more you take action whenever you're tempted to put something off, the stronger the habit of doing so will become. Over time, the temptation to procrastinate, always present, will seem less and less powerful. Taking action will become easier and easier.

Having said the above, it's important to realize that no change can happen without your commitment to *making* it happen. To that end, I urge you to do more than just read *The Procrastination Cure*. Apply the material to your daily life.

Use *Part I: Why We Procrastinate* as a checklist of sorts to recognize the specific triggers that cause you to procrastinate.

Use *Part II: 21 Ways To Beat Your Inner Procrastinator* as a playbook in curbing the habit. Incorporate each tactic, one at a time, into your daily process. I'm 100% confident you'll be pleasantly surprised by the results.

Use *Part III: When Procrastination HELPS You To Get Things Done* as an opportunity to experiment with active procrastination. The practice doesn't work for everybody. But the only way to know whether it works for you is to try it.

This book offers *actionable* advice on nearly every page. It's purposely light on theory and heavy on practical tips. Here's how I recommend you go through it...

First, given that you're reading this, it's safe to assume you've read *The Procrastination Cure* in its entirety. You're familiar with the core concepts involved with curbing the procrastination habit.

Now, revisit each section. Be an "active" reader as you do so. As you reread *Part I*, write down your personal procrastination triggers. Take action on the suggestions I've included with them to lessen their influence on you.

As you reread *Part II*, apply each of the tactics. As we discussed earlier, proceed slowly. Incorporate one tactic per week, and allow it to become a habit before moving on to the next one.

As you reread *Part III*, think of ways to slowly integrate active procrastination into your day. Again, do so as an experiment so you can determine if it works for you.

Here's the bottom line: you have the ability to make positive changes in your life. You hold the reins. You're in control. *The Procrastination Cure* offers a simple roadmap that'll take you from your current circumstances to your desired destination. All that remains is for you to follow the map.

It won't be easy. Nor will it happen quickly. Most of us have enabled our inner procrastinators throughout our lives. So overcoming the habit might take a significant amount of time. Expect to face internal resistance as your mind struggles to maintain the status quo.

Eventually, if you apply the tips and suggestions provided in this book, you'll find that you're increasingly less inclined to put things off. The temptation to do so will always be present, but you'll be less beholden to it.

That's when you'll know that you've won the battle.

Before you read *The Procrastination Cure* a second time, commit to breaking the procrastination habit. Make a personal pledge to apply every tactic I've recommended. I'm confident you'll notice marked change in your tendency to procrastinate within a few weeks. You'll also notice that taking action will make you feel more empowered. Over the course of a few months, you'll start to look forward to tackling tasks and projects that once filled you with dread.

I'd love to hear from you as you experience this metamorphosis. Reach out to me at <u>damon@artofproductivity.com</u>. Tell me about your personal triumphs and share your minor missteps.

DID YOU ENJOY READING THE PROCRASTINATION CURE?

~

I'm deeply humbled that you've finished reading *The Procrastination Cure*. You undoubtedly could have spent the time doing something more fun and exciting, but decided to stick with me throughout this book.

Thank you.

Learning to control my inner procrastinator has improved my life in many ways. I'm certain you'll enjoy the same experience. My hope is that the tips and tactics I've shared throughout this book will play a role in that experience.

If you enjoyed reading *The Procrastination Cure*, would you do me a favor? Would you visit Amazon and leave a quick review, noting something you liked about the book? Your review will encourage others to read it.

On a side note: I have several action guides planned for the coming year. I have a feeling you're going to love them. If you'd like to be notified when I release them, and take advantage of early discount pricing, join my mailing list. You'll receive my 40-

page PDF ebook titled *Catapult Your Productivity! The Top 10 Habits You Must Develop To Get More Things Done.*

You can join my list at the following address:

http://artofproductivity.com/free-gift/

You'll also receive my best productivity and time management tips via my email newsletter. I'll show you how to make the most of your time, adopt positive habits, and design a truly rewarding lifestyle!

All the best,

Damon Zahariades
http://artofproductivity.com

ABOUT THE AUTHOR

Damon Zahariades is a corporate refugee who endured years of unnecessary meetings, drive-by chats with coworkers, and a distraction-laden work environment before striking out on his own. Today, in addition to being the author of a growing catalog of time management and productivity books, he's the showrunner for the productivity blog <u>ArtofProductivity.com</u>.

In his spare time, he shows off his copywriting chops by powering the content marketing campaigns used by today's growing businesses to attract customers.

Damon lives in Southern California with his beautiful, supportive wife and their frisky dog. He's currently staring down the barrel of his 50th birthday.

OTHER BOOKS BY DAMON ZAHARIADES

∼

**The Joy Of Imperfection: A Stress-Free Guide To Silencing Your
Inner Critic, Conquering Perfectionism, and Becoming The Best
Version Of Yourself!**

Is perfectionism causing you to feel stressed, irritated, and chronically
unhappy? Here's how to silence your inner critic, embrace imperfection,
and live without fear!

∼

**The Art Of Saying NO: How To Stand Your Ground, Reclaim Your
Time And Energy, And Refuse To Be Taken For Granted (Without
Feeling Guilty!)**

Are you fed up with people taking you for granted? Learn how to set
boundaries, stand your ground, and inspire others' respect in the
process!

∼

**Morning Makeover: How To Boost Your Productivity, Explode Your
Energy, and Create An Extraordinary Life - One Morning At A Time!**

Would you like to start each day on the right foot? Here's how to create
quality morning routines that set you up for more daily success!

∼

Fast Focus: A Quick-Start Guide To Mastering Your Attention, Ignoring Distractions, And Getting More Done In Less Time!

Are you constantly distracted? Does your mind wander after just a few minutes? Learn how to develop laser-sharp focus!

~

Small Habits Revolution: 10 Steps To Transforming Your Life Through The Power Of Mini Habits!

Got 5 minutes a day? Use this simple, effective plan for creating any new habit you desire!

~

To-Do List Formula: A Stress-Free Guide To Creating To-Do Lists That Work!

Finally! A step-by-step system for creating to-do lists that'll actually help you to get things done!

~

The 30-Day Productivity Plan: Break The 30 Bad Habits That Are Sabotaging Your Time Management - One Day At A Time!

Need a daily action plan to boost your productivity? This 30-day guide is the solution to your time management woes!

~

The Time Chunking Method: A 10-Step Action Plan For Increasing Your Productivity

It's one of the most popular time management strategies used today. Double your productivity with this easy 10-step system.

Digital Detox: The Ultimate Guide To Beating Technology Addiction, Cultivating Mindfulness, and Enjoying More Creativity, Inspiration, And Balance In Your Life!

Are you addicted to Facebook and Instagram? Are you obsessed with your phone? Use this simple, step-by-step plan to take a technology vacation!

For a complete list, please visit

http://artofproductivity.com/my-books/

Made in the USA
Middletown, DE
12 July 2023